THE CAMPUS SCENE, 1900–1970

OTHER BOOKS BY THE AUTHOR

Chinese Cooking for American Kitchens

Chinatown, U. S. A.

One Man, One Vote

Improving College Teaching

Whose Goals for American Higher Education

THE CAMPUS SCENE, 1900–1970

Changing Styles in Undergraduate Life

by
CALVIN B. T. LEE

DAVID McKAY COMPANY, INC.

New York

THE CAMPUS SCENE, 1900–1970

A list of photo credits appears on page x.

Library of Congress Catalog Card Number: 70–120171

MANUFACTURED IN THE UNITED STATES OF AMERICA

VAN REES PRESS • NEW YORK

FOR

Christopher and Craig

PREFACE AND ACKNOWLEDGMENTS

THE CAMPUS SCENE, 1900–1970 has been in the works for a number of years. It developed out of an occupational hazard required of deans, to explain the present generation to alumni. But it was also a labor of love. No one in his right mind could be an academic administrator unless he profoundly believed in youth—past, present, and future.

For a dean of a college in the late Sixties, it was difficult enough to keep up with normal work, amid sit-ins, confrontations, and curriculum reform, much less try to write a book. It was completed only with the assistance of many. My wife, Beverly, not only tolerated late, late evenings, and lost weekends, but also read many volumes of college histories to cull out materials for the book.

Numerous friends and acquaintances were subjected to interviews about their college days, and they in turn subjected their friends across the country to the same procedure. They were generous with their insights as well as their enthusiasm. I was overwhelmed by the enthusiastic cooperation of the many colleges and universities that supplied photographs for the book.

I am indebted to friends who read the earlier drafts and commented on them, particularly to Alan Brody for his many helpful suggestions.

A special word of thanks is owed to John Burke, Jr.—classmate and loyal friend—who read and criticized the manuscript and also helped select the photographs. Similarly, my editor, Elliott W. Schryver, was a constant source of support.

My secretary, Nadine Houston, lived with this book through its many drafts cheerfully and loyally. Other members of my staff who helped were Aleta Downs, Carole Smith, Colleen Kohler, and Patricia Washburn.

Finally, I want to thank Audrey Evans, who edited draft after draft of the manuscript, helped to select pictures, spent many hours of research in the library, and agonized with me through it all.

CALVIN B. T. LEE

College of Liberal Arts
Boston University

CONTENTS

Photographs follow page 114

PHOTO CREDITS

Associated Press, 105

Barnard College, 79, 80, 81, 83
Bennett College, 17 through 37 inclusive, 38, 41, 42, 45, 58
Boston University, 39, 47, 48, 49, 108

Chronicle of Higher Education, 107
Columbia University, 43, 64, 65
Culver Pictures, Inc., 78

Deseret News Photo, 61
Dillard University, 51

Kentucky State College, 1, 14

Loretta Heights, Denver, 40

Marietta College, 109
Michigan State University, 15, 16
Montana State University, 59, 71
Mount Holyoke College, 14, 75

Oberlin College, 52, 54, 62, 63, 104

Purdue University, 56, 57

Skidmore College, 4, 11, 89, 91
Stanford University, 72
Sweet Briar College, 7, 8, 9, 12, 90

Temple University, 95

Underwood and Underwood, 5
United Press International, 43, 50, 53, 66, 97, 98, 99, 102, 106
University of Denver, 87, 88
University of Kentucky, 60, 76, 77, 86
University of Michigan, 3
University of Oklahoma, 2
University of Texas, 55
University of Utah, 82

Vassar, 10

Wellesley, 6, 44, 84, 85
Wide World Photos, Inc., 67, 68, 69, 70, 73, 74, 93, 94, 96, 100, 101, 103

INTRODUCTION

COLLEGE days, our own college days, are very personal. Whatever we may recall about them, our favorite college-day stories, our reminiscences, whether they were joyful and happy or grim and bitter—those days influenced our lives in a major way.

It wasn't just the friends we made, the courses we took, or the professors we admired. The experience was more than that, and the additional element that made it so is difficult to identify. I like to call it ethos.

Each college generation has an ethos of its own—its distinguishing character, tone, or guiding beliefs. Although there may be differences from college to college or region to region during the same period, there is almost always an overriding mood, rhythm, or style that determines the character of college life in any period. Thus, the first decade or so of this century was dominated by sentimentality and innocence. The classes of the Twenties were affected by the Jazz Age and Prohibition, giving them a legend of being mad, bad, and glad. The Depression imposed a tone of soberness on the classes of the Thirties. Following the Second World War, the returning G.I.s upset all campus tradition by crowding the campuses with wives, children, and even pets. The Fifties' classes are known as the Silent Generation dominated by McCarthy, the Cold

War, Korea, and the Organization Man. And the Sixties, a very complex and active period, included commitment and dissent. All of us were in some way affected by the action and passion of our particular time.

Nevertheless, none of these periods can be simply categorized in one word. There were always leitmotifs in the web of activities we call college days. Political radicalism on campus, for instance, can be traced back to the 1900s, a fact that we tend to forget. A loudly touted revolution in manners and morals is always taking place, and prohibition against alcohol in the Twenties can be effectively compared to the illegality of marijuana in the Sixties.

In addition to the leitmotifs, there are the counterpoints. The otherwise grim Depression period was also the time of elaborate college hoaxes and fads like goldfish swallowing. And the straitlaced Silent Generation of the Fifties sought release through panty raids. At the same time, the wildness of the Twenties often obscures the equally strong desire for a "return to normalcy."

Then there is the alumnus's perception of later generations. Change, whether for good or for ill, frequently causes a momentary shock in those who perceive it. It is not surprising that we have not always been sympathetic to the youngsters filling our seats. Around 1910, alumni watched in horror as colleges began to permit social dancing on campus. They were repelled by the marches staged by college women in the late Teens for women's suffrage. The intensity of alumni reaction to the revolution of manners and morals on the campuses in the Twenties was surely equal to the feelings expressed today. On the other hand, graduates of the Thirties who were politically involved looked with disdain at the Silent Generation of the Fifties because of their lack of idealism and commitment.

Everyone uses his college days as a personal reference

point for past, present, and future. For each of us, our
college days are memorable. Over the years, we have em-
bellished our college-day stories, fitted ourselves more
firmly with the ethos of the period, and perhaps have lost
sight of the context from which we, too, were rebelling. It
is not the purpose of this book to smash these myths.
Indeed, it may help to give us a new perspective of them.

CHAPTER I

THE GOOD OLD DAYS, 1900–1920

ALUMNI of the first decade and a half of the twentieth century did not become sentimental with age—they grew
up on sentimentality. In tune with the tempo of their times,
college men, accompanied by tinkling mandolins, sang about
unrequited love, good girls gone wrong, and broken hearts.
The music of this period ranged from sentimental ballads
and waltzes like "Good Night, Ladies" and "Moonlight
Bay" to the more lively tunes that followed in the second
decade, like "Oh, You Beautiful Doll" and "Five Foot Two
—Eyes of Blue." Tin Pan Alley sold over a million copies
of sheet music of "Let Me Call You Sweetheart" and "Down
By the Old Mill Stream." Other campus favorites included
"Just a Song at Twilight," "After the Ball Is Over," and
"Tah-Rah-Rah-Boom De-A." The "coon song" was becom-
ing increasingly popular. Carried over from the late 1800s
by Harry Von Pilzer, it offered tunes such as: "Alexander,
Don't You Love Your Baby No More?" and "What You
Gon' to Do When the Rent Comes 'Round?"

But a change was taking place in music. By 1910 the
quickening of the tempo in popular music and dance reflected the speeding up of the country. Keeping pace with
Henry Ford's Model T, popular music moved into ragtime—
at first, a change more apparent than real, by the simple

process of syncopation, shifting the accent to the off beat. By the second decade of the twentieth century, college students were dancing the Turkey Trot or Grizzly Bear to the tune of "Alexander's Ragtime Band" and "Everybody's Doing It Now." So important was the music to campus life that at Princeton University, Kenneth Clark, who had never played on a varsity team, won a varsity letter for producing the tunes "Princeton, That's All" and "Going Back to Nassau Hall." By World War I, jazz had taken the place of ragtime as the dominant musical force on college campuses.

These changes in music and dance on campus appear innocent enough, but they took place only after intense criticism, student revolt, and finally concession by the deans, faculty, trustees, and alumni. Social dancing, it should be recalled, was not permitted on most college campuses during the first decade or so of the twentieth century. Colleges were still in the Victorian period when coeducational functions on campus were very rare and meticulously chaperoned. The new music was criticized not only because the tempo was different; the lyrics were attacked as suggestive and risqué. The dances were considered too loose, too fast, and required partners to hold each other in a close embrace. From the latter dilemma came the famous "two-foot rule" requiring that the distance separating the sexes must be two feet, and apparently some young ladies took to carrying a ruler.

The lives of Deans of Men and Deans of Women in these early days were occupied with evolving regulations for appropriate dances of the college students. Unapproved dances were denounced in press and pulpit. Latin dances, particularly the "Tango Pirate," were considered to be smooth, sinister, foreign, and full of immoral designs. Objectionable dances other than Latin were considered to be of Negro origin. And a convenient catch-all admonition was that song, dance, or general behavior was "improper."

Among the dances banned by Deans of Women were the Grizzly Bear, the Bunny Hug, the Tango, and the Boston Dip. At Columbia College the prom committee put a ban on the Turkey Trot around 1912. Across Broadway at Barnard College, the question of "one stepping" was debated until 1915, when the class ball committee had two "one steps" for every waltz and even one Tango! At Wellesley there was a good deal of controversy, particularly over the Boston Dip. But it was often pointed out that this dance and other new dances were danced at the White House wedding of President Woodrow Wilson's daughter. At Carleton-Headley trouble flared in 1910 over the rule against social dancing on campus. According to the administration, the rule banning dancing was based "not on moral grounds, but merely on those of expediency." The faculty finally adopted a new rule that allowed some off-campus dancing with *parents' permission,* and it wasn't until 1918 that the first dance actually took place on campus. Among the women's colleges some acted faster than others. Smith girls were allowed their first mixed dancing promenade as early as 1894, and Vassar had its first in 1897. But Mount Holyoke didn't relent until 1913, after the student body had threatened to wear black all the time.

College days were carefree, innocent, and fun. For the generation of college students from 1900 to the beginning of the First World War, higher education was still primarily for the elite (or at least moderately elite), and purposeful revolutionizing of society was far from most of their minds. Yet it should not be assumed, as older nostalgic alumni tend to do, that ferment was not part of this student generation, that change was not taking place, and that tradition prevailed entirely. The style and manner of bringing about change seem tranquil compared to the confrontation politics of the late Sixties. Yet change was taking place on the cam-

puses, and the good old days at the beginning of the century
—within the context of the times—were as exciting and
eventful as they were rich.

Rousing events, camaraderie, class pride, and school
spirit were the signs of the day, and fraternities and social
clubs filled a social and emotional need. While the *laissez-
faire* attitude of college administrations toward the non-
academic activities of student life prevailed, the Greek-
letter societies and other social clubs assumed a great deal
of the responsibility for the feeding, housing, and general
welfare of students. Particularly at geographically isolated
colleges and denominational schools, the fraternities often
provided the only source of entertainment and excitement
for the students.

Fraternity rushing became intense at some institutions.
At Cornell at the beginning of the century, freshmen were
met at the railroad station by a mob of men yelling, "Hey,
Frosh, save a date for ABK." Hailed from house to house,
he was then pledged within two or three days. Membership
was frequently awarded to the student according to the
wealth reflected in his clothes. The desirable qualities of a
candidate did not particularly include brains, especially
in sororities. Suzanne Wilcox, in an article entitled "The
Conduct of College Girls" published in *The Independent*
on August 7, 1913, recounts a story in which a sorority
girl, after a long and serious discussion with a young man,
was reprimanded by her sorority sisters for dwelling on
serious matters. "You must talk frivolously to fraternity
men—or you will ruin our reputation."

Because of the great importance of fraternities, an anti-
fraternity movement, particularly in the South, developed
at the turn of the century. The Mississippi legislature

banned secret societies at state colleges in 1912 and kept this law on the books until 1926. Fraternities, according to the accusing lawmen, "encouraged dissipation, led to a waste of money, discouraged study and scholarship, interfered with the work of the literary societies, destroyed college spirit, fostered cliques, and caused social ostracism of non-members." Southern and Western Populists attacked both fraternities and sororities as being anti-democratic and exclusive. Members were chosen for candidacy, the orators declaimed, for their good clothes, good looks, good family, and good income. The development of a special caste at public institutions was highly objectionable. Initiation ceremonies were mystical, highly secret, and often required vows that were execrable to certain religions and creeds. Some put the pledges through tests of courage that occasionally backfired, resulting in maiming and death. A less than manly boy, carted off in the dark of night to a distant place and harassed on his return, was likely to succumb to fright that disqualified him.

In the East, even more exclusive organizations evolved alongside Greek-letter societies. At Yale the famous secret senior societies of Skull and Bones and Scroll and Key had greater prominence than most fraternities. Similar senior societies appeared at Columbia, Wesleyan, and even as far west as the University of Michigan. Blatant social stratification took place on Harvard's "Gold Coast" and in the eating clubs at Princeton. So entrenched was this system separating the well-to-do from the have-nots that one of Woodrow Wilson's appeals to voters was that while he was president of Princeton he used all his influence to abolish the eating clubs, though without success. Significantly, the creation of small communal units for all freshmen took place at Harvard in 1914 when three freshmen halls opened with the stated purpose of a "more natural, friendly and democratic basis of college life."

Ostensibly to create a sense of class spirit, freshmen were often required to wear beanies and to be subjected to hazing by sophomores and upper classmen. Often these class rivalries were climaxed by the Frosh-Soph Rush, a contest between the members of the two classes, causing much of damage to body, limb, and property. At Syracuse University the contest between freshmen and sophomores was called the "salt rush." Considered too rough, the combat was replaced by the "flour rush"—involving bags and stockings of flour instead of salt. In one of the most popular contests, a six-foot pushball placed in the middle of the field awaited the hundreds of freshmen and sophomores on either side who attempted to push the ball across the opposite goal line. Many a student went home with abrasions, bruises, and contusions—if not broken bones. Another common battle between the two classes was the contest for the first to reach the top of a greased flagpole. The prize for all of this battling was, of course, that the freshmen might win the privilege of removing their beanies. Spirits rose high in the college days of the early 1900s, and Soph-Frosh competition sought to enhance this feeling.

If fraternities, secret societies, and eating clubs promoted social stratification, big-time college football, in its own way, offered individualism and democratic opportunity. One British observer wrote:

The sons of Czechs and Poles can score there, can break through the barriers that stand in the way of the children of "Bohunks" and "Polacks." And although Harvard may secretly rejoice when it can put a winning team on to Soldier's Field whose names suggest the Mayflower, it would rather put on a team that can beat Yale . . .

Thus Daly was elected captain at Harvard in 1900 and Pierkarski of Penn made All-American in 1904.

Big-time college athletics began their rise about 1880, and by the turn of the century wealthy and enthusiastic alumni supported the construction of large stadiums, salaried coaches, athletic scholarships, and winning teams. The great zeal simmered down for a while in 1905. For in that year, 18 college football players were killed, and President Theodore Roosevelt, a great fan himself, focused national attention on the situation when he invited the athletic directors of Princeton, Yale, and Harvard to the White House and asked them to remove "foul play" from the game.

In those days football was a simple game of brute force, of mass formations: the flying wedge, the revolving wedge, occasionally varied by an end run behind three-man interference. No substitutions were made except when a man was too groggy to stand up. Helmets and modern shoulder pads and guards had not yet been developed; the main safeguard was that the field was ploughed. Slow as it was by modern standards, it was an exciting game to watch.

Football was abolished in 1905 at Columbia because the faculty considered it "an academic nuisance"; ironically, rowing (far more physically taxing) then became the big sport at Columbia. In 1915 football was permitted again but excluded games with Yale, Harvard, Princeton, Cornell, or Penn for five more years in order to discourage overemphasis on competitive football.

At Stanford in 1906 football was outlawed on the grounds that it was too rough and professional. Stanford and the University of California both officially switched

from football to rugby. Even at the smaller colleges like
Tufts, there was general concern over questionable recruiting, financial practices, and downgrading academic requirements for players. The Intercollegiate Athletic Association of the United States was established as part of a
"systematic attempt to improve the situation in intercollegiate athletics."

In 1907 Michigan left the "Big Ten" to join the "Ivy
League," a loose confederation of Eastern universities
and small colleges. Michigan did poorly with this competition.

In *Outing Magazine* a sportswriter claimed that the anti-
football movement had gone too far. His solution was
simply to confine each student to one sport and forbid
long trips. He maintained that more participation of
students in more sports would lessen the attention on one
team and a few star players. In *The Educational Review*
another author pointed out that students could not be
blamed for the athletic craze. Thirty to forty thousand
people come for a big game at Yale, Harvard, or Princeton.
Newspapers devoted excessive attention to the glory of
spectacular players. General publicity was perhaps just as
responsible for the situation as were the colleges.

College faculties even at this early date were appalled
to discover that the worth of an institution was often determined in the minds of the public, including the alumni,
by the number of athletic games it could win. Over the
whole country, academicians slowly and reluctantly realized that American life was demanding that its universities
provide mass entertainment and vicarious thrills. College
faculties tried to control abuses by rules, the most common
being that no man could play ball if he was delinquent in
his studies.

Collier's magazine in 1909 devoted an issue to "Is Football Worthwhile?" and found in interviews with college presidents that almost all were in favor of retaining football but changing some of the rules to lessen the chance of serious accidents. At the University of Kentucky in 1912, students passed a resolution to "suppress violence and rudeness at intercollegiate games." In his history of Tulane, Dyer wrote, "In virtually every institution of higher learning in the country, pre-World War I years saw random physical exercise transformed into team play and then team play assumed, in the minds of great masses of the public, an importance greater than that of professor in classroom."

Drinking after the big football games was, of course, one of the campus highlights. In 1913 the Washington *Star* reported that after a Georgetown versus University of Virginia game "the police worked overtime gathering up nearly a hundred young drunks who had to put up ten dollars or sleep in a cell . . . In front of one thirst parlor a line of police waited until midnight when the lights were made dim and about twenty drunks spilled out toward the curb."

California combined Eastern college traditions with those of pioneer gold-rush days. At the University of California, students had their "wet" celebrations away from campus—often ending up smashing dishes, throwing steins, and sliding under the table. At Berkeley, kegs of beer were rolled to the top of the hill for the all-night annual "beer bust." Stanford finally banished liquor from the campus after a drunken student got into the wrong fraternity house and was shot as a burglar.

According to one 1903 investigation of an "eastern university center," 90 percent drank in the freshman year, 95 percent in the senior year, 35 percent drank heavily, and 15 percent became drunkards. Harry S. Warner reported that "at Yale drinking is recognized to so great a degree that clubs have their tables at the barrooms . . . and in some of the bars students carve their names on the tables. The table tops are preserved as souvenirs of the year on the walls of the saloon and new tops put on the tables for another year of names."

From 1910 until the war, the colleges became increasingly aware of the liquor problem. In socially influential colleges, smaller institutions, and denominational colleges, concern and questioning created some temperance. Especially in central and Southern states, local and state laws were passed to prohibit liquor. Abstinence became socially acceptable. Some fraternities even went dry and student movements rose to prohibit liquor. By 1911 Cornell boasted that a new period of morality was developing. According to its college alumni magazine, "drinking and sexual impurity had been cut fifty percent during the last seven years in large well known eastern universities." The reasons for this "wonderful moral and religious advance" were in great part the increased interest in clean sports. At Yale in 1915 the senior class voted (115 to 101) to discontinue liquor at the graduating party and at their future class reunions. The Intercollegiate Prohibition Association promoted study and discussion of the problem in hundreds of colleges.

For some, perhaps, there was motivation for so-called clean living. Corporations such as General Electric, Westinghouse, and Bessemer Steel were demanding "purity of life" on the part of prospective employees. To some extent, ambitious college students were gearing themselves to please businesses and corporations.

From the turn of the century until World War I, the grandeur of college life reflected, for the elite, the fun of fraternity life, the rise of collegiate football, and the alumni reference point of the "good old days." But it was not really as uniform as all that. Land-grant colleges, created by the Morrill Act of 1862, gave the less well-to-do an opportunity for college training, undermining the established elite. At the University of New Hampshire in 1919, 60 percent of the students were the children of farmers, 25 percent entirely self-supporting, and 50 percent partially supported. Girls learned to cook in home economics and worked in restaurants during the summer. Yet fraternities and sororities flourished at the University of New Hampshire. Fifty percent of the men and 60 percent of the women belonged.

Some private colleges also served the less well-to-do or children of parents moving up the social ladder. At Carleton, students prior to 1900 were from the industrial middle class, later from professions—physicians, bankers, and lawyers. In 1911 Nazarene University, a struggling college on the West Coast, charged a registration fee of three dollars, tuition of twenty dollars per semester, and room and board per week was four dollars and twenty-five cents. A corner room in the dormitory cost an extra twenty-five cents per week.

Nevertheless, the college tone of this period was dominated by the well-to-do, reflecting the life style of older established colleges. At Bryn Mawr, maids for the students were housed in the top floor of the dormitories. The genteel tradition prevailed in college life.

The finishing school and seminary had been the goal of most girls, but the emerging academic woman of the early 1900s was quite a new breed. Higher education for women dated back scarcely a generation, and the college-educated woman was for many a distinctly unsettling phenomenon. She was described as masculine, unattractive, aggressive, and a damned nuisance, but nonetheless she had a style of her own. Many outraged conservatives decried the new young woman. But H. L. Mencken (who used the word flapper before the real flapper appeared) liked her, described her best, and with her, her whole milieu:

The American language, curiously enough, has no name for her. In German she is der Backfisch, in French she is l'Ingenue, in English she is the Flapper. But in American, as I say, she is nameless, for Chicken will never, never do . . .

Observe, then, this nameless one, this American Flapper. Her skirts have just reached her very trim and pretty ankles; her hair, newly coiled upon her skull, has just exposed the ravishing whiteness of her neck. A charming creature! . . .

Well, well, let us be exact: let us not say innocence. This Flapper, to tell the truth, is far, far, far from a simpleton. . . . Life, indeed, is almost empty of surprises, mysteries, horrors to this Flapper of 1915. . . . She knows exactly what the Wassermann reaction is, and has made up her mind that she will never marry a man who can't show an unmistakable negative . . . She has read Christabel Pankhurst and Ellen Key, and is inclined to think that there must be something in this new doctrine of free motherhood. She is opposed to the double standard of morality, and favors a law prohibiting it . . .

This Flapper has forgotten how to simper; she seldom blushes; and it is impossible to shock her. She saw "Damaged Goods" without batting an eye, and went away wondering what the row over it was all about. The police of her city having prohibited "Mrs. Warren's Profession," she read it one rainy Sunday afternoon, and found it a mass of platitudes . . . She admires Strind-

berg, particularly his "Countess Julie." She plans to read
Havelock Ellis during the coming summer . . .

As I have said, a charming young creature. There is something
trim and trig and confident about her. She is easy in her manners. She bears herself with dignity in all societies . . . There is
music in her laugh. She is youth, she is hope, she is romance—
she is wisdom!

A clothing revolution for women occurred around 1913.
Corsets went out, no longer considered necessary. A slit
appeared in the side of skirts up to the middle of the calf
and even to the knee (revealing, of course, a delectable
expanse of leg). Supposdly it was designed to make it less
difficult to get in and out of cars.

When skirts finally were raised six inches above the
ground in 1919, *Vogue* observed that "not since the days
of the Bourbons has the woman of fashion been visible to
far above the ankle." When, in the following year, another
three inches came off the hemline, *The New York Times*
commented that it was "far beyond any modest limitation."
However, for the pre-war coed, modesty in dress was still
firmly and strictly the rule. Girls wore hobble skirts, high
collars, and ribbon bows in their hair. Variations of the
shirtwaist were everywhere to be found. For cold weather
they wore mackinaws or English Norfolk blazers and buckskin golfshoes. Bobbed hair was just beginning to be
fashionable and girls still carried fancywork bags and an-
noyed professors by patting the bead work in class.

College women may or may not have been proper, but
they certainly weren't docile. In 1900 a college suffrage
group was founded at Radcliffe by Miss Maude Wood. In
1908 suffrage groups from college campuses in fifteen
states came together to form the National College Woman's
Equal Suffrage League. Officers and board members were

graduates or faculty members from Bryn Mawr, Barnard, Radcliffe, Smith, and the Universities of Wisconsin, Chicago, and California. At Mount Holyoke, interest in suffrage increased slowly until about 1910, at which point Mount Holyoke became militant over the issue. In 1911 they organized a chapter of the Equal Suffrage League and in 1912 twenty-five students and five faculty members particiapted in a Boston parade.

At Wellesley in 1911, after five states had given the vote to women, an informal poll of students showed the students to be against the enfranchisement of women. However, a year later they had changed their minds. Campus radicalism took to other issues as well under the leadership of Vida Scudder, an English Literature professor and a member of the Socialist Party. In 1900 when the first Rockefeller gift was made to Wellesley, Scudder and other faculty members protested accepting money from the profits of the Standard Oil Company. In 1912 when A.F. of L. workers were striking in the nearby town of Lawrence, Professor Scudder and Professor Ellen Hayes of the Astronomy Department spoke at a meeting of the Progressive Woman's Club urging them to send their children away when the strike became violent and protesting police handling of women in the strike.

But the feminist spirit was not confined to political issues and suffrage. The heyday of female team sports was taking place. Vassar girls became very enthusiastic about intramural sports: track and field, field hockey, and basketball. Wellesley was famous for its crew teams. But even though girls participated in sports, they were not to give up their modesty. The girl's basketball team in 1910 at the University of Michigan wore middy blouses and full bloomers over black stockings. For the yearbook the dean ordered that "the figure must not be shown in photographs," so the team photo was taken with the girls lying down on the floor, elbows on floor, chins in hand, facing the camera.

The youngest President of the United States, Theodore Roosevelt, took office in 1901 after the assassination of McKinley. Energetic, robust, and only forty-three years old, T.R. was as popular with the college youth of that era as John F. Kennedy was five decades later. Followed briefly by a single term of William Howard Taft, the end of this college generation coincided with the aloof idealism that marked the administration of Woodrow Wilson, former professor and university president.

Intellectually, culturally, socially, and politically, America was shaken out of the Victorian age and into a new American mode. Intellectually—especially through William James, George Santayana, and John Dewey—America was defining a philosophy of its own. Culturally, for better or for worse, America developed its own style, turning away from British and European tradition. For the young rebels, protesters, and writers, this era of both the little magazine and mass magazine offered publication to divergent political views and new literary trends, which of course influenced the student and professor avant-garde of the day. Little magazines such as *Poetry, The Little Review,* and *The Masses* were developing. Southern intellectuals started the *South Atlantic Quarterly* and the *Sewanee Review.*

The most exciting years of *Poetry* were the first ones, 1912 to 1917, when debate over free verse and imagism seemed vital. Among those whose earlier poems appeared were: Robert Frost, Wallace Stevens, T. S. Eliot, William Carlos Williams, D. H. Lawrence, and Ezra Pound. During the formative years of *The Little Review,* founded in 1914, Nietzsche, Bergson, anarchism, and psychoanalysis were recognized and discussed. In 1912 Floyd Dell and Max Eastman decided to make *The Masses* a rebel literary magazine. It became the first important literary voice of the left-wingers and provided the domestic inspiration for the so-called "proletarian" movement of the sociologically-minded Thirties. During its life it published the early work of Louis Untermeyer, Carl Sandburg, William Rose Benét, John Reed, and Walter Lippmann.

The *New Republic,* starting in 1914 under the editorship of Herbert Croly, called for revival in education, literature, and government. Other magazines that appealed to campus intellectuals included *Smart Set* under Mencken and Nathan and *The Seven Arts* under the editorship of Van Wyck Brooks and Randolph Bourne. Carried over from the nineteenth century were magazines like *Century, Harper's Magazine,* and *Scribner's.* While muckraking was bringing success to *McClure's,* respectable reform was debated in *The Nation* and *Harper's Weekly.*

To speak of the Progressives as a single movement is to grossly simplify the period and the political philosophies of the main contributors. Nevertheless, one can agree with historian Richard Hofstadter that at the heart of Progressivism was "the effort to restore a type of economic individualism and political democracy that was widely believed to have existed earlier in America and to have been destroyed by the great corporation and the corrupt political machine; and with that restoration to bring back a kind of morality and civic purity that was also believed to have been lost."

Historian Henry May remarked:

The Young Intellectual regarded the dominant kind of progressivism, with its emphasis on throwing out the crooks and its small business loyalties, as a bore and something of a fraud.

Yet they had been attracted by the Bull Moose Progressive party, as interpreted by Herbert Croly. Its demand for leadership, its occasional use of the language of scientific management, made it seem promising. Few of the Young Intellectuals, like everybody else, found themselves impressed by his swift and masterful grasp of power during his [Roosevelt's] first two years as President.

The young intellectuals of this era were much more deeply affected by the pragmatism of William James and the social and intellectual reconstruction of John Dewey than by popularized Progressivism.

A new kind of social criticism in the pre-war period produced on the campuses several literary and political figures who would dominate twentieth-century thinking. Harvard's poets included Conrad Aiken, e. e. cummings, and Malcolm Cowley. Walter Lippmann was president of the Harvard Socialist Club in 1909; other new critics emerging from the campus were Van Wyck Brooks, John Reed, and Harold Stearns. Princeton's crop included F. Scott Fitzgerald and Edmund Wilson. Yale graduates of this period included William Rose Benét, Thomas Beer, Waldo Frank, Sinclair Lewis, and Archibald MacLeish. These men were to be very influential in changing the dominant set of ideas in the late Teens as well as the Twenties and Thirties. Out of the good old days came this new generation of intellectuals.

The First World War had a profound effect on American colleges. By the mid-Teens every phase of student life was subjected to heavy criticism from such diverse types as businessmen, high school principals, disgruntled professors, and Cassandras of the social order. Robert Lincoln Kelly wrote in *Scribner's Magazine* in January 1918:

The college engaged in a disgraceful scramble for numbers and money, it was said; it was dominated by athletics; it was expensive, undemocratic, irreligious. College men were impudent, ill-trained, knew nothing well, were not fond of work, had no definite end in view; they could not even spell or add a column of figures. The institution was a parasite sucking out red blood from the body politic.

Colleges were also pummeled as the centers of pacifism. Many college presidents and professors had allied themselves on the side of peace, and even at land-grant colleges where military training was available to students, the numbers enrolled were small and warlike activities were perfunctory.

But the campus reaction to military preparation was by no means uniform. In 1915, two years before the United States entered the war, the University of Michigan faculty senate vote as well as a student poll favored military training on campus. In March 1917, 3,369 male students were polled as in favor, 632 opposed to military training, yet the Board of Regents did not authorize compulsory military drill. But all opposition to military drill on the part of the Regents was finally overrun a month later when President Wilson and Congress issued the Declaration of War.

The responsiveness of college men and the colleges was startling. Student enlistments became so high that great concern arose over whether the colleges would be completely depopulated. Eight hundred left Yale for military service, 700 departed from the University of Michigan before the end of the year, and so it was at hundreds of colleges throughout the country. In response to this demonstration of patriotism, colleges granted academic credit for the remainder of the year even when the students had left in midsemester. The universities of Wisconsin and

Michigan even awarded degrees at special commencement exercises at Army training camps.

The statistics of college enrollment show the extent of the losses in student bodies. In a study of 113 colleges of liberal arts by the U.S. Bureau of Education, the institutions enrolled 60,596 men students in 1916, and in 1917 they enrolled 48,090. More surprising perhaps was faculty enlistment. Colleges lost as much as a quarter to a half of the faculty. Princeton and Yale sent 40 to war; Northwestern, the University of Louisville, and the University of Chicago each furnished 50; while 74 went from the University of Wisconsin.

At many colleges students raised money and prepared dressings. At many small agricultural colleges, the war effort included the volunteer participation of students in raising their own food and cutting wood for fuel, because food and coal were scarce. Some students graduated early and others got credit "in absentia" when they quit classes to help farmers in the war effort.

At the women's colleges the students worked on relief projects. Two years before the United States entered the war, students at Wellesley began to organize adoption of French orphans and to aid Edith Wharton's hospital in France. In 1917 the presidents of Smith, Vassar, Wellesley, and Mount Holyoke met to discuss the war effort. Free electives in war-related subjects included courses in typing, wireless, telegraphy, and gardening. Many students went to France as nurses or for canteen and recreational work.

As James Wechsler pointed out in *Revolt on the Campus,* "The war invaded the curriculum, the laboratory, and virtually every university facility." A twelve-page supplement to the catalogue outlined "war studies" at Reed College. Yale provided a new three-year course on subjects relating exclusively to "military career, as an alternative to the regular college course."

The curriculum was revised at many colleges. James Wechsler described Dean Paul Boyd's "revisions" of the curriculum at Kentucky University:

With fitting flourishes he [Dean Boyd] depicted the evidences of "virility" in each field. Philosophy "made plain the roots of present day Teutonic madness." English professors presented their material with an eye to service "as a tool for the transfer of exact information."

"War chemicals" became the major pre-occupation of the Chemistry Department. "History," he explained quite succinctly, "was made more definite." In the Art Department "principles of camouflage" were the source of primary concern. And agriculture, home economics, engineering and law all found plenty to do that contributed toward the one great problem of organizing a nation for war.

The Princeton *Alumni Weekly* boasted that "every day Princeton becomes less an academic college and more a school of war." In response to the request of the War Department, President Thomson of Ohio State replied, "The faculty and trustees pledge you their loyal support in your leadership. The resources of the university in scientific and research laboratories and in men will be at your command." And so it was for most universities and colleges.

Not since the Civil War had the American colleges faced such a crisis of low enrollment aggravated by the high cost of fuel and food. To counteract this crisis as well as to develop a continuing cadre of college-educated men for the military, the War Department in 1918 announced that it would establish a Student Army Training Corps on the college campuses. Provision was made for the induction of 200,000 men who hopefully would provide the Army with doctors, chemists, and other highly trained men and officers. At first the S.A.T.C. plan was voluntary, but later became compulsory when the draft age was lowered to 18, and the S.A.T.C. plan was successful in increasing enrollments at a number of colleges. At Cornell, where the entire college had been crippled by the war, the S.A.T.C. brought 1,700 students inducted as soldiers when they arrived on campus. Some institutions that did not have S.A.T.C. units were almost completely stripped of men.

S.A.T.C. changed the style and customs of each member college. The tone of the campus was set by Army dormitories. Empty fraternity houses were converted into canteens and barracks. Schools that had frowned upon the use of tobacco on campus not only witnessed its wide use but also its sale on college property. Professors went to work at the sound of the bugle, and many of them trod in fear of violating some rule that would (at that time) make them liable to court-martial. Time-honored academic traditions were broken. Subjects in all liberal arts curricula were dropped: Greek, German, Logic, Botany, Archaeology, Philology, Sociology, and a few other subjects not on the program of "war aims." Mathematics, Physics, and Chemistry received great emphasis, and some professors whose courses were not in vogue were compelled to brush up on their mathematics in order to teach courses in that field.

But all was not always well with S.A.T.C. on campus. S.A.T.C. students were not always recruited for academic potential or excellence. Professors complained of the contrast between pre-war students and the S.A.T.C. recruits. Relations between professors and military instructors were strained. At the University of Michigan, all students were turned out for drill and told to disregard any instructions from the faculty on peril of court-martial.

The S.A.T.C. program was short-lived, and by December 1918 orders were issued to disband the units. But the program had a continuing impact on college enrollments even following the war. Criticized for requiring only enough college work to destroy the curriculum and not enough military drill to make the soldier, the S.A.T.C. nonetheless gave thousands of young men their first contact with college life, and many finished college even after they were discharged from the S.A.T.C.

The fall after the Armistice brought unprecedented enrollments to colleges, with increases ranging from 10 to 60 percent. This era of wide expansion led to a further democratization of higher education.

CHAPTER II

THE TWENTIES: MAD, BAD, AND GLAD

THE Twenties became notoriously the decade of the young. Mark Sullivan wrote, "The Twenties, reversing age-old custom, Biblical precept and familiar adage, was a period in which, in many respects, youth was the model, age the imitator. On the dance-floor, in the beauty parlor, on the golf course; in clothes, manners, and many points of view, elders strove earnestly to look and act like their children, in many cases their grandchildren." If the daughter started the flapper style, it was her mother who kept it going.

F. Scott Fitzgerald's *This Side of Paradise,* published in 1920, has been described as "an opening gun in the pro-youth, pro-freedom, and anti-Puritanism campaign," and to a large extent it established the sterotype that was to cling to an entire generation of college youth. Historian William Leuchtenburg wrote, "The mood of the country was hedonistic; Omar Khayyám's quatrains took the colleges by storm. The ideal of hedonism was living for the moment, and if one can isolate a single spirit which permeated every segment of society in the postwar years, it was the obliteration of time." And to obliterate time there were such crazes as crossword puzzles, Mah-Jongg, flagpole sitting, and Marathon dances.

College days of the Twenties have been depicted as mad, bad, and glad. The decade was dubbed the Jazz Age, the Flaming Twenties, and the Era of Excess. Yet, when Warren G. Harding was running for President in 1920, the phrase that most appealed to the mood of the country was "back to normalcy." As Mark Sullivan explained it, "It was a yearning for 'the time of peace wherein we trusted'—not meaning merely for peace in the sense of absence of war, but for peace in the sense of serenity, for a state of things in which it was possible to feel trust, to rely upon permanence." Presidents Harding, Coolidge, and Hoover gave that appearance of peace, serenity, and permanence to the national scene, but social change came with accelerating speed.

Technological advance strongly marked the times. It was in 1920 that Studebaker stopped making horsedrawn wagons; the automobile was here to stay. Radios appeared in every parlor. The first feature sound film, *The Jazz Singer,* starring Al Jolson, was produced in 1927. And in the same year Charles Lindbergh made man's first solo flight across the Atlantic.

The Twenties fortified scientific inquiry in the face of prejudice and doctrine. It was during this period that the "monkey trial" of John T. Scopes tested the Tennessee law forbidding the teaching of evolution. The court drama was really a showpiece for two of the country's greatest trial lawyers, Clarence Darrow and William Jennings Bryan, pitting the last bastions of Fundamentalist belief against scientific truth.

Jazz was the music, the saxophone the instrument, and the Charleston the dance. Every campus had its own student jazz band, and the music reflected the feelings of this student generation.

As J. A. Rogers says:

Jazz isn't music merely, it is a spirit that can express itself in almost anything. The true spirit of jazz is a joyous revolt from convention, custom, authority, boredom, even sorrow—from everything that would confine the soul of man and hinder its riding free on the air. The Negroes who invented it called their songs the "Blues," and they weren't capable of satire or deception. Jazz was their explosive attempt to cast off the blues and be happy, carefree happy even in the midst of sordidness and sorrow. And that is why it has been such a balm for modern ennui, and has become a safety valve for modern machine-ridden and convention-bound society. It is the revolt of the emotions against repression.

At the same time, the ballad still remained popular. A survey by the *Woman's Home Companion* of the ten greatest songs of the Twenties in the opinion of 370 musicians produced the following titles: "Tea for Two" (1924), "I'll See You in My Dreams" (1924), "The Man I Love" (1924), "When Day Is Done" (1926), "Ol' Man River" (1927), "Russian Lullaby" (1927), "My Blue Heaven" (1927), "Lover, Come Back to Me" (1928), and "Star Dust" (1929). But nostalgia strikes all those who today recall the tunes "It's Three O'Clock in the Morning" (which was played by many bands as the closing melody, instead of "Goodnight, Ladies"), "Blue Skies," and "Toot, Toot, Tootsie Goodbye." The latter was from *The Jazz Singer* (1927).

At the fraternity houses they were singing the University of Maine's "Stein Song" that Rudy Vallee popularized in the late Twenties and early Thirties, and "Makin' Whoopee," which Eddie Cantor made famous. In 1923 "Yes, We Have No Bananas" was sung everywhere, and

"Show Me the Way to Go Home" (1925) ruled the rest of the decade. The most prophetic little song of all was "I Can't Give You Anything but Love, Baby" (1928), sung with feeling among the students after the Crash.

The Jazz Age arrived on the campuses across the country at different times. The Jazz Age didn't hit Michigan until 1925 and wasn't in full swing until 1927. Here the student immediately after World War I had "a more dignified attitude toward himself and the university." Men's suits were back to blue serge again along with thick sweaters without turtlenecks and felt or cloth hats. As changing styles moved westward, wags began to quip "the feminine waistline changed so fast that students didn't know, when reaching for a girl's waist whether they would trip her or choke her." Styles for college girls included jersey wool Bramley in green, rust, and fawn, and flapping galoshes (thus the name flappers). Rouge and powder were usual but not lipstick. By the end of the decade racoon coats were selling for up to $400 with as many as six flask pockets. As for the classic accessory to the coon coats, some observers considered the ukulele a worst pest in the post-war era than the mandolin had been twenty years previously. At the University of Michigan sororities kept strict rules on hours and liquor, and fraternities made an effort in that direction, but there was general non-observance. Because so many students were killed in accidents, a strict ban was put on student cars in 1927. In a few cases, students were given a choice of "your college career or your car" and after careful consideration chose the car; they were given twenty-four hours to leave the campus.

Smaller, isolated colleges also remained conservative. At

Carleton-Headley immediately after the war "there was no sudden nor dramatic change in social life in the Twenties, but rather gradual deepseated changes in the attitude and flavor of the college . . . more sophistication or pretentiousness, if you will," according to the history of the college. Fashions did come to Carleton, however, in the form of raccoon coats, short skirts, and bobs. But student social life was almost the same as in the Teens except for dance music. They continued their favorite pastimes of skating, tobogganing, walking, swiming, and fishing.

Perhaps the literature of this period, dominated by now famous names, changed the thinking of America more than any other element. True, the light reading was light. As Allen Churchill says in *Remember When,* "On college campuses, the young hungrily perused the magazine *College Humor,* with its bittersweet stories by Katherine Brush and its daring ones by Lynn and Lois Montross."

The best sellers of those years were of headier stuff, and they created a climate for the college intellectual even into the Thirties. Sinclair Lewis wrote both *Main Street,* which jarred parents, and *Babbitt,* which, with T. S. Eliot's *The Waste Land,* shook up the young. Thomas Mann's *The Magic Mountain,* Fitzgerald's *The Great Gatsby,* Dreiser's *An American Tragedy,* and Hemingway's *Farewell to Arms* greatly influenced young minds. For the revolution of viewpoint, perhaps no other books roused the questioning of values as much as Aldous Huxley's *Point Counter Point* and *The Modern Temper* by Joseph Wood Krutch, whose humanistic influence at Columbia University extended over the next three decades as well, then for two more decades when he became a naturalist of the Southwest.

Dennison College reported that "no less than a moral revolution was in progress throughout American life, and a Baptist college in an Ohio valley could not escape its effect. For instance, in 1915 every student in the college belonged to the YMCA. By 1923 little more than one-third of the members showed interest. There was a general easing of social rules."

Changes took place more slowly at many of the state universities and colleges. The dean of the University of North Dakota in 1920 put a ban on "cheek to cheek dancing, unnecessary clinging, cuddling or dancing the shimmy." At one point there was even a student committee called the Women's Senate of Secret Observers to report the above offenses. But these rules and others applied only to official on-campus affairs, and because of the increasing amount of off-campus housing, automobiles, and informal dating, the rules were difficult to enforce.

The institutional historian of the University of Rhode Island boasted that "Rhode Island students never descended to the depths of depravity that characterized social life at Brown and Pembroke, where bare-knee kissing enjoyed a mysterious vogue." President Edwards of Rhode Island crusaded against modern dancing and influences that "pertained to the lust of the flesh, the lust of the eye and a pride of life."

At Ball State, smoking was not a problem because, as the school newspaper wrote, "there has never been a ruling by the faculty against smoking on the campus and will probably never be necessary because in most cases a man has enough respect for his alma mater to refrain from smoking while on campus."

Smoking by women was a problem at some women's colleges. At Wellesley the girls were not allowed to smoke "within the Township of Wellesley and Natick." So down they went to the town line to sit on the stone wall in large numbers to smoke in a protest that led to the creation of a "smoking room" in 1928. At Bryn Mawr smoking rules were taken off the books by the mid-Twenties. Vassar and other Eastern Women's colleges followed suit within two years. Barnard College had no problem with smoking and drinking; according to the administration, students had good sense with regard to drinking, and the college had never taken a stand against smoking at all. The Barnard student council set up smoking areas, and as public opinion accepted women's smoking in public so did Barnard, calmly and effortlessly, because there was no embarrassing earlier position to abandon.

Rules were also changing with regard to the necessity of chaperons. In 1920 it was considered a major concession for Wellesley to allow its girls to go unchaperoned in groups of two or more to the movies in the evening. Soon girls were allowed to go on Sunday and evening drives without chaperons. And before anyone knew it, students went as far as to organize a "syndicate for blind dates— fifty cents a date, twenty-five cents additional if the dates called afterwards and one dollar for a dinner date." All the funds collected by this syndicate were properly donated to the college's semi-centennial. On the other hand, social life at Sweet Briar wasn't deeply affected by the Twenties. An alumna wrote, ". . . our amusements in the Twenties were unsophisticated. Walking was still one of the chief diversions."

The films of the era, still in the throes of Valentino, De Mille, Charlie Chaplin, and ever more glorious Westerns, realistic war films, and Biblical dramas, finally struck pay dirt in filming the behavior of the day. Some contend that such movies created the ethos of the time. Clara Bow was every college boy's dream girl. The slicked-down hair of the boys not only appeared on the screen heroes, but hair products were advertised in the school yearbooks —Stacomb and Brilliantine. Striped flannels, ukuleles, flivvers and bearcats, wild parties, hip flasks, cocktails, petting, the Charleston and the Black Bottom, and the long-handled cigarette holders created the clichés that the fast crowd thought it should live up to and the timid may have thought were real. The supposed sophistication of the film industry in its first grand decade depicted the new American freedoms of college life in *The Freshman and the Flirt* (Harold Lloyd), *Prodigal Daughters* (Gloria Swanson), *The Plastic Age* (Clara Bow). Other titles were: *The Quarterback, Our Dancing Daughters, Our Modern Maidens, The House of Youth, The Perfect Flapper.*

In spite of the stereotype of the Twenties that there was a great deal of drinking and sex on campus, many magazine articles and studies at the time indicated that these activities were over-exaggerated. *The Ladies' Home Journal* ran a series on "Fashion in College Morals" that included studies of the University of Chicago, Wisconsin, Stanford, Harvard, and Princeton and offered the conclusion that drinking and sex were confined to a small minority of the student body. A survey by *The Christian Science Monitor* found that only four out of 114 colleges reported an increase in drinking after Prohibition went into effect in 1919.

The Literary Digest in 1926 published the results of a questionnaire on college student drinking that it submitted to the heads of 213 institutions and a hundred editors of college publications. The almost unanimous opinion was that drinking in the colleges as a whole had decreased during Prohibition. Hip flasks had become taboo in most institutions, and unroarious cocktail parties were no longer a favorite form of celebration. The significant difference between the college editors and the college heads was that the editors criticized the Volstead Act as creating a temptation.

According to a poll taken by the *Yale News,* a student publication, drinking at Yale had not declined, and Professor Irving Fisher testified before the Senate Sub-Committee on Prohibition that the prevailing sentiment in the Yale student body was wet, that as much as 80 percent of the students were not in sympathy with Prohibition, but that the number of discipline cases in which drinking was a factor was very much smaller than before Prohibition. "There is less drinking than before Prohibition," said *The Alumni Weekly,* "but what there is, is more serious; there is more drinking of 'hard liquor'; public disorders arising from too much drinking are fewer but more serious when they do happen." A poll conducted by the Harvard *Crimson* favored a modification of the Prohibition law. The editor of the *Crimson* reported that there was a certain amount of drinking in the rooms and clubs and a little at dances; but drinking was not carried on ostentatiously, and hip flasks had never become a fad. A somewhat different view came from Williams College, where, wrote E. Herbert Botsford of the Williams *Alumni Review,* "the attitude of the undergraduate body is strongly in favor of law and order," though "undoubtedly a majority would vote for a modification of the present law."

Princeton editors could not agree whether there was actually more or less drinking there than before Prohibition. One editor wrote that there was very little drunkenness, although this "does not apply to the weekends, when there are important affairs going on, such as House Party weekend, weekends of big games (especially football) and Prom times." On those occasions "there is frequently drunkenness." "But it seems unlikely," said the writer, "that there is more drinking at these times than before Prohibition. Certainly there is not the tacit acceptance of a drunk at any dance or class prom which we are told was traditionally the case in pre-Prohibition time."

Samuel Carter of *The Princetonian* asserted in out-and-out fashion that drinking had increased, if anything, since he entered college, and that roughly 70 percent of the men in his class drank. From the undergraduate viewpoint, he said, the whole law "is altogether wrong, and has had a distinctly detrimental effect on the colleges; and, unfortunately or childishly unfair as it may seem, the undergraduate will not observe the law."

Crediting his college with more sobriety than it knew when he entered it five years previously and much more than was the case before Prohibition, H. Lincoln Houghton, editor of *The Bowdoin Bear Skin,* of Bowdoin College, Maine, presented the interesting view that the sobriety was not entirely due to Prohibition. "There has been," he wrote, "a corresponding abatement of other forms of dissipation, of sexual immorality, of gambling, of hazing, and all that sort of thing," which he thought was "far more due to the fact that the college is now attracting men of not necessarily higher caliber, but certainly more serious tempers."

In the Middlewest, sentiment in favor of Prohibition was fairly universal among the colleges, according to *The Literary Digest*'s poll. Some drinking was reported, but this was laid to the bad example set by the elders, particularly by returning graduates, and to the "spirit of daredeviltry" innate in a certain type of adolescence.

At Michigan there was some resentment against the charge that the moral fiber of studenthood had become weakened and some admission that there was drinking among students. President C. C. Little noted that several influences complicated the situation and made a sound estimate of the effect of Prohibition difficult. These influences were: the increase in the size of the student bodies, the use of the automobile by undergraduates, and the reduction of time and distance between colleges and large centers of population by the automobile.

In the Far Western states, the survey found that student sentiment was strong for law observance in regard to Prohibition. President Ray Lyman Wilbur of Stanford University said that the liquor problem "is about one-tenth of what it was" during his student days there; he remarked that the "magnification of infractions of the Prohibition Law has given a false and exaggerated picture." The liquor problem had not presented itself at California Christian College, Los Angeles, but President Arthur Braden had opportunity to observe the effects at the State University across the street, and it was his "candid opinion" that there was much less drinking there than there was among students during his own student days in a "great university in the East."

As to the Southern states, *The Literary Digest* wrote:

If the college heads speak truly, the mint julep and eggnog will soon be known no more. The frost is off the glass and the cherry is on the tree. The bowl which once flowed with rhetoric, fond recollection and faint regret is now filled with nuts and fruits, which contain no conversation. Thus, we are led to believe, have their own and the National Prohibition Laws changed the old order and set a new one on the ways. The South has changed in many respects, not more, perhaps, than in departing from the method with which it welcomed and sped the parting guest and in which it regaled itself as occasion and season required. A new state has crept upon us. Cotton is still king, the Colonel still smokes, and chews a little; but, we are led to believe, he and his sons have given up their Bourbon.

The general view of the heads of Southern colleges would seem to agree with the emphatic remark of one of the officers of Washington and Lee University:

> Since the close of the World War and the advent of woman's suffrage there has been a prevalent epidemic of revolt against every form of tradition, convention, ecclesiastical, social, and moral restraint of which the present demand for liberty to buy and drink liquor as any one wishes is in no sense a result but only an additional proof.
>
> I regard the present outcry in and from certain sections of our non-American population, especially along the Atlantic seaboard, as mainly a definite, well-organized and liberally financed propaganda to break down all legal restraint against the distribution of intoxicants and other similar laws restricting personal liberty in the interest of ethics and morality.

If the Twenties is depicted as the decade of mad, bad, and glad, then what was a sin in college? *Nation* magazine (May 20, 1925, Vol. 120) conducted a poll at the University of Texas during the years 1919 to 1921. The ratings opposite are based on arithmetical averages. Number 1 represented what the student thought was the worst offense, and so on for the rest.

This same test was given to students at the Universities of Chicago, Kansas, Wisconsin, and Colorado, and at Columbia. The ratings in these Northern universities were the same as those at Texas, with the exception of one practice. In the Northern universities sabbath-breaking was placed in the fourteenth or fifteenth rank, as relatively unobjectionable. At Texas it was placed in the eighth or

	Rankings by	
Practices	*Men*	*Women*
Sex Irregularity	1	1
Stealing	2	2
Cheating	3	3
Lying	4	4
Drinking	6	5
Gambling	5	6
Vulgar Talk	7	7
Sabbath-breaking	9	8
Swearing	8	9
Gossip	13	10
Selfishness	10	11
Idleness	11	12
Snobbishness	12	13
Extravagance	14	14
Smoking	15	15
Dancing	16	16

ninth rank, which would seem to indicate a sectional difference between the North and South.

The actual excesses of the Twenties may well have been exaggerated, perhaps by the tantalizing images created by F. Scott Fitzgerald, but a profound intellectual and emotional change was taking place in the minds and attitudes of the college generation. As suggested by Mark Sullivan, the attitudes of the younger generation were not molded wholly by the war, nor were they as new as they thought. The causes went as far back as Darwin in the 1860s, and included the doctrines of Freud about sex that hit America in 1910, the reading of the hedonistic quatrains of Omar Khayyám, the jeering at conventionality that Bernard Shaw kept up for more than a generation, and the novels of

H. G. Wells. All these influences and many others, growing cumulatively, came to a climax in the Twenties. To
these were added the effect of the Russian Revolution. The
ferment could not help but affect young Americans greatly.
The "younger generation" as well as the "lost generation"
took these new ideas and themselves most seriously.

One of the most perceptive observations of these college
years appeared in an article entitled "Ours Was the Best
Generation" by Gene Shuford:

Even in the beginning we were unique. Conceived in an
irreligious period, we held the most romantic of faiths—that of
salvation by sex. Freud was our high priest: Lawrence the god
who thrust us toward an escape from the bald daylight of current
rationalism. Through Lawrence we beheld man crouched at the
edge of the pitiful circle of light, around him all the horror of
the dark. Yet the light, the ecstasy were there; and unreasonably
we expected our newly found godhood to rub on our humanity.
Beneath our fashionable cynicism we wanted the ecstasy without the bitterness . . .

Eventually we realized this; the magic fire with which Lawrence
had illuminated sex guttered out in our own feeble experience.
We believed that Lawrence had failed, that the race had failed;
and that the symbol of the final chapter of *The Rainbow* was
false . . .

In short, we were still pretty adolescent and sexually incompetent. For all our Lawrence and Ellis and Freud we floundered
badly, had our flights and met our disasters, were no less bitter,
and found our suffering no less tragic or real. Indeed, some suffered more. Confused by heavy intellectual paraphernalia, the
inept missed both ecstasy and agony, and rising shamefacedly
from their experiences, questioned naturally, "Well, is that all?"
Such frustration broke down many a romance and marriage and
left scars that were years in healing.

Yet we had all the newly learned ritual of the science—psychology and biology; we had read hundreds of case histories of

everything from exhibitionism to sadism; we believed that the intellectual could replace the outworn moral control of our emotions. What we failed to realize was that science is but an approach to reality, and not reality itself; biology or psychology is a candle, but not the floodlight of emotional experience. Such was the fatalism and defeatism we inherited from the generation known as "lost." Their sense of futility flooded our thought stream, but it did not flow into our blood. Our generation had not experienced the War; they had. We had not been exiled; they had ... People, writers and others, had told us such things between the delightful interludes or dabbling in sex and liquor and going to college and stepping into any number of jobs and finding all sorts of chickens in all sorts of pots; but we really didn't know anything, and Paris was just a far-off, romantic place where immortals like Joyce and Hemingway had lived; and Spain was merely a marvelous place for fiestas filled with pleasantly drunken aficionados attending bullfights and not a land where women are soldiers, where they mutilate the dying, and place the prisoners in front to be shot or burned alive by exploding gasoline tanks.

No, underneath we really thought we were all right; that man in general was all right; that the shadows were merely to make it all more interesting. Nothing had come along really to test us, and we were soft. Of course sex wasn't going well because most of us were too serious and really didn't know anything and dreaded any disciplining life offered us; but we hadn't the slightest suspicion of our complete immaturity. Had the boom not ended when it did, we should have all been putrescent before we had a chance to ripen. You see, we really didn't know anything at all.

The Twenties was a period in which people lost their fear of Hell and their interest in Heaven. One critic of the lack of religion on campuses complained that, "The Department of Philosophy, in a spirit of intellectual conceit, is encouraging a type of liberalism and criticism which is little short of the rankest infidelity . . . Conscience is deadened, the distinction between right and wrong is made less real." The Twenties became the Period of the Psyche as Freud's sexual theories were popularly disseminated after the war.

Students talked knowingly of "neurosis," "libido," "fixation," "repression," and other such terms as if they were simple ideas. The Sears, Roebuck catalogue offered *Ten Thousand Dreams Interpreted* and *Sex Problems Solved*. Books offering "psychology" included: *The Psychology of the Poet Shelley* as well as *The Psychology of Selling Life Insurance*. Hypnotism was a going rage.

Dean Christian Gauss of Princeton, in contrasting the 1890s with the 1920s, said:

I confess that I do not know precisely what a neurosis is. I console myself with the feeling that in this I am like many undergraduate contestants for the prize, and some of their elders. In my time in college we never discussed neurosis. All we knew was a mysterious malady—nervous prostration. Fortunately it never attacked us, but once in a while we heard that one of our instructors was down with it.

It was not a commonplace ailment like scarlet fever or Bright's disease or consumption. It gave distinction to a professor's leave of absence. It set him apart; for we still tended to regard as superior anyone who had nerves. Now everybody has them and in varying fashions. The old generic "nervous prostration" has disappeared from the vocabulary of the educated. "Neurosis" is a better and a newer word. Above all, it is scientific, and any bright sophomore knows that if you wish to shut off the twaddle of some drolling conservative, the thing to do is to use a scientific term on him. It acts like a sedative. Tell him he has an Oedipus complex or that he is a hypomanic and he will be frightened and subside. In this respect times have changed all around, and, whether they have new perversities or not, undergraduates today, with the rest of us, certainly have new words to conjure with.

The theories of Freud and Jung had an impact on writers, particularly in developing new techniques for exploring human motivation. Eugene O'Neill used Freudian themes in *Desire Under the Elms* (1924), *Strange Interlude* (1928), and *Mourning Becomes Electra* (1931). The "stream-of-consciousness" technique became famous through James Joyce's *Ulysses* and was used by William Faulkner in *The Sound and the Fury* (1929).

Only the collegiate elite, of course, discovered James Joyce's *Ulysses* early in the Twenties—it was published in 1922 in Paris—and the tradition-breaking language was as unrestrained as anything published in the late 1960s. The court case over its publication in the United States in the Thirties made historic the pronouncement that "literary merit" saved some books from being impounded as pornography.

At any rate, smuggling became widespread among college youth. One Princeton undergraduate, the son of a judge, was badgered by his father for not taking off his coat during a sweltering passage through customs inspection coming home from Paris. How could the lad be expected to confess that beneath his vest he was carrying the many pages of *Ulysses?* At the University of Chicago, a copy was later circulated widely under the counter by the university bookstore rental service, until bought for a "swindle" by the editor of this book—in 1934. The final thirty pages, Molly Bloom's thoughts in bed, were blackened with many hundred college fingerprints.

On the campuses the general cultural revolution was reflected in a lessened control over sex. Eight hundred college girls met at a conference to discuss petting: whether or not? how far? The consensus was: Learn temperance in petting, not abstinence. As Lloyd Morris observed: "The word 'neck' ceased to be a noun; abruptly became a verb; immediately lost all anatomical precision."

F. Scott Fitzgerald said of the post-World War I generation, "Here was a new generation . . . grown up to find all gods dead, all wars fought, all faiths in men shaken." Similarly John F. Carter wrote in *The Atlantic Monthly*, "The older generation has pretty well ruined the world before passing it on to us. They gave us this thing, knocked to pieces, leaky, red-hot, threatening to blow up; and then they are surprised that we don't accept it with the same attitude of pretty, decorous enthusiasm with which they received it way back in the Eighties."

There were two manifestations to the student rebellion. One was the revolt in manners and morals, which was a revolt "without benefit of Lenin." As James Wechsler wrote:

It betrayed no concern for politics, politicians or the future destiny of mankind. Firmly convinced that the world was a maudlin, unhappy, oppressive place to inhabit, the lieutenants of the movement proposed to make the best—or the worst—of it . . . Nothing had been saved in the war to save everything. Confused, disappointed, duped, the "younger generation," or a substantial part of it, determined to set out for itself along these paths most repugnant to its elders. They did so deliberately, maliciously, but with an earnestness graphically descriptive of their plight. They had been cheated and deceived because they were credulous; now they proposed to be too sophisticated to permit further deception.

The other manifestation after the First World War according to Wechsler "sought to sing of renewed hope, to discover, in the ruins, a promise of a better future." This was the manifestation of the often forgotten political movement.

Soon after the war, there grew up the Intercollegiate Liberal League. Early in 1922 the League merged with the National Student Committee for the Limitation of Armaments and its periodical, *The New Student,* came into existence. It announced in its first issue, "Students hold within their careless, unmanicured fingers the preservation of our civilization. Our elders know it. They tremble at the casual way we grasp our inheritance." For these students, President Harding's "return to normalcy" was not to be achieved without vast readjustments and social change. In October 1923 *The New Student* maintained, "With all respect to the older generation, some of us become more and more certain that they cannot feel the chaos as we do." Wechsler said of their position, "It was further deduced that all evil was the product of age and that youth was the obvious antidote. That was the crux of their belief. Stated in its most extreme form, it held that a man might be of some use to the community until he was thirty years old, but after that he was automatically aligned with the legions of darkness."

The New Student didn't have a blueprint: "All that we know is that as students we had certain dissatisfactions; that others seem to have similar ones . . . We can't tell exactly what is coming . . . when there is a common student consciousness which reaches across from campus to campus and includes a sufficient number of thinking students, any action will shape itself."

The period following World War I was one of "The Big Red Scare." Millions of Americans seriously thought that a Red revolution might begin in the United States. To these

millions, Bolshevism was precisely equated with the growing union movement. These were the days when front pages
of the newspapers shouted the news of strikes and anti-
Bolshevist riots. It was a day when the Vice President of
the United States cited as a dangerous manifestation of
radicalism in the women's colleges the fact that the girl
debaters of Radcliffe upheld the affirmative in an intercollegiate debate on the subject: "Resolved, that the recognition of labor unions by employers is essential to successful
collective bargaining."

Censorship and a growing mood of general intolerance
also appeared on campus. A lecture by Scott Nearing in
1922 at Clark University was halted by President Wallace
W. Atwood after five minutes. The Barnard Student Council protested the attempt to "quarantine students from ideas"
by the censorship of speakers. A number of professors at
various private church-related institutions were discovered
to be Jews and thus judged ineligible to teach. A debate
about limiting the number of Jewish students was taking
place at a number of colleges, including Harvard. Temple
University dropped a teacher who was suspected of atheism
and liberalism. Mercer University dropped a professor of
biology whose "attitude toward certain basic evangelic
beliefs" prevented him "from presenting the facts of science
in such a way as to strengthen the faith of the students in
those doctrines which evangelic Christians held to be most
essential." *The New Student* criticized the newly founded
American Association of University Professors: "The rout
of the A.A.U.P. seems to be general . . . Dismissals keep
going on and the Association's Committees inquire whether
it has been done politely."

Norman Thomas wrote in 1923 that "the prophet of the
minority of our youth is Mencken, not Marx." Mencken
said that his goal was "to combat, chiefly by ridicule,

American piety, stupidity, tinpot morality, cheap chauvinism in all forms." Mencken's coverage of the Scopes trial caused his enemies to take notice of him and try to counterattack. The effect of H. L. Mencken and his magazine, *The American Mercury,* was of such magnitude that a more conservative member of the University of Chicago faculty said, "The one thing that makes me fear for the future is the number of our students who read *The American Mercury;* on the campus you see it under every arm; they absorb everything in it." And a number of ministers were talking at colleges so that students would "be saved from the beliefs preached by H. L. Mencken."

Nonetheless Mencken denounced college students for their readiness to "consecrate themselves, on getting their degrees, to the mortgage bond business and the development of refined suburbs." Yet the college intellectuals recited him like scripture. But one critic complained that "college liberalism finds it so much easier to laugh at the booboisie than to understand or work with the proletariat, to criticize Main Street than to make an effort to recreate it."

As for the fear that college students were becoming Communists, Dr. Glenn Hoover pointed out that the average college student was the son of Babbitt and was upholding the family tradition. The Twenties were dominated by the image of the "rah-rah" college boy and girl. If their exploits in drinking and sex were exaggerated, they were at least content to create a myth. There was little room for student radicalism. Toward the end of the career of *The New Student,* editor Douglas Haskell wrote:

The huge difference between 1927 and 1922, when *The New Student* was modestly incepted, is that there is no doubt of American prosperity and comfort. That changes the whole map and the whole enterprise. It occurred to me . . . that the whole effect we were after hung together with the idea that there was going to be grand changes in the country. There aren't. Therefore, reluctantly it must be admitted that nearly all the revolts we began fostering in colleges have degenerated into mean scuffles ... Where we used to dream of new faiths and new communities developing out of colleges and flowering through a thankful country, now the main hope is that students will be less bored by lecturing ...

Wechsler later wrote:

The whole temper of the intellectual movement had become one of despair—despair in its surroundings and in the insufficiency of its own efforts. On the campus, neither the "revolt in manners and morals," the romantic idealism of the early *New Student,* nor the bitter shafts of the Menckenites had provided any satisfactory answer to those who, for one reason or another, could find no adjustment in the world of boom. As Walter Lippmann said in *A Preface to Morals*: "What most distinguished the generation who have approached maturity since the debacle of idealism at the end of the war is not their rebellion ... but their disillusionment with their own rebellion."

For all the ferment the new ideas brought from abroad and popularized by men like Mencken were still in the process of being absorbed into the American psyche. This state of semi-absorption was to give the Twenties a curious flavor that appeared to border on superficiality. It remained for the Thirties to make these new concepts uniquely American. Frances Warfield's description of her college life illustrates the semi-innocence and semi-sophistication that characterized her era:

Completely illiterate when I entered college, I emerged almost entirely unscathed. I spent four years sipping cultural soothing-syrup, and was graduated amid small excited squeals and admiring hushed comment on my coruscant intellectuality. In my home town I am now referred to as an educated woman, a college woman. It's great: All my life I shall be eligible as a reader of papers before Browning Societies and Thursday Afternoon Shakespeare Circles. My young suitor? I have forgotten his name. He is probably a first-rate dental architect.

Let no one think that I learned nothing in college. I learned to use the best brands of canned chicken, sports clothes, and cosmetics. I learned to pluck my eyebrows. I learned the earmarks of culture—a well-modulated voice, well-regulated enthusiasms, the attentive strained rapture of intelligent listening which renders vacuity impregnable.

But I never learned anything that would upset me. I was told enough about writers, scientists, philosophers, and the like to last me all my life, without ever reading the men themselves. I learned that Emerson was a transcendentalist, that Pasteur took all the bugs out of milk. I learned to pronounce Nietzsche's name. That, for any woman, is enough. I learned the plain and fancy catchwords of erudition and how to apply them.

My library seemed embarrassingly small. But I found I needed no books whatsoever; that I needed instead sweaters, sports skirts, rubbersoled shoes, pennants, felt cushions in college colors, family photographs, stunt books, wicker chairs, tea-sets, electric toasters, Maxfield Parrish pictures. No one cared whether or not I knew anything. Every one asked if I were interested in debating, class banners, class meetings, self-government, sunrise hikes, crew tests, college songs, humorous stunts, the Bird Club, St. Hilda's Guild.

I found that money was not a standard of comparison and that a large number of the students were poor. Some were even working their way. It was important, socially, that one come from a good prep school, have correct table manners, and be a Gentile. If one's family came to visit and was presentable, it was a slight asset but no more. For every one soon discovers that almost all families are queer.

... There are the literary ones (girls). They shed tears over Hardy and Meredith and the "Rubáiyát" and the Irish playwrights and read Pater, the nineteenth century poets, Sherwood

Anderson, W. B. Maxwell, F. Scott Fitzgerald, Max Beerbohm, Shaw, A.S.M. Hutchinson, Hugh Walpole, all indiscriminately. They adore Irish literature because it is chock full of brogue and leprechauns. They think Russian writers are frightfully morbid. Some write poetry.

There are the public-spirited ones. They grow interested in current events, in strikes and socialism and immigration. They read the newspapers and talk together intensely, reconciling Plato with prohibition, Karl Marx with open plumbing. They know, of course, as much about the relation between capital and labor as they do of the private life of minute tapioca.

There are the musical ones who play much Chopin and no Bach. There are the artistic ones who do landscape-gardening. There are the dramatic ones who look forward to opening a Little Theatre in a deserted barn just outside Peculiar, Minn., and putting on "Riders to the Sea."

Those who have held steadfast to social service grow earnest and take to carrying around large books of sociology and economics. They learn that sometimes babies have no papas, and that if these babies belong to poor people they constitute a Social Problem. They prate about standards of living, the Jukes, and the Mendelian ratio. Subconsciously most of them yearn to marry and escape settlement houses forever, and for that reason they speak often and unfavorably of men and of marriage.

And so passed college life in the mad, bad, glad Twenties, the golden age of Joe College. The prosperity of the country was such that young men could be sent to college to have a good time and not worry about the future. Even at the state universities and colleges where the students were less affluent, the tone of campus life was light.

The collegiate mood of the Twenties was affected not only by expansion of the pre-World War I traditions of big-time college football and fraternity life, but also by a freer attitude toward the opposite sex and more open (though not necessarily more widespread) use of alcohol.

The period of the hip flask coincided with the hero worship of such collegiate football stars as Red Grange of the University of Illinois and the Four Horsemen at Notre Dame.

Alumni supported the construction of lavish new fraternity houses and filled the stadiums on Saturdays as the fervor for collegiate football reached its highest. And afterwards, alumni as well as students would retire to enjoy fraternal camaraderie and revelry. Although the amount of liquor consumed and the extent of sexual activity may have been over-exaggerated, the campus scene of this college generation was nevertheless typified by fraternity and sorority houses, dances, and parties.

For all its talk about Freud and the profound intellectual changes that were beginning to take place, this generation of college students was marked by a charming superficiality, a semi-sophistication, and a semi-innocence. In short, it was an era of fun, self-indulgence, and optimism.

CHAPTER III

THE THIRTIES: HARD TIMES AND SOMBER STUDENTS

THE Jazz Age ended dramatically with the stock market crash of 1929. By 1932 the Depression caused unemployment for thirteen million people and wages were 60 percent less than in 1929. Between 1929 and 1934, college placement offices reported that between 50 and 85 percent of their male graduates were unemployed. Streams of college graduates were volunteering for the Army for what the New York *Post* called "grub, prosaic grub." Law school graduates taught elementary school. Department stores were hiring college graduates as sales clerks. Some recent graduates, who were lucky enough to find funds to scrape along, went to graduate school rather than face the jobless business world. A *Harper's Magazine* article in that same year said, "In many respects the post-1929 college graduate is the American tragedy. He is all dressed up with no place to go . . ." In 1935, 150,000 students with degrees were emerging into a world that did not want them.

At the University of Michigan a thousand students left in 1930, another thousand hung on, some almost starving to get their degrees, and then faced unemployment. For college students menial part-time jobs were often easier to find than full-time employment. At Duquesne University (Pittsburgh) many tried to get part-time jobs in the steel mills and factories, and to survive, one student became an undertaker's helper. Colleges endeavored to help students by giving them campus jobs as janitors, switchboard operators, or locker room attendants. Students worked as meatcutters, plumbers, and tailors. At least one Cornell student became a gigolo! On the other hand, "Let" Philbin literally fought his way through college as a welterweight professional boxer in 153 fights. Trapped foreign students found themselves peddling novelties from their native lands.

The Federal Emergency Relief Administration was started in 1934 to give Federal aid to students in the form of employment. Funds were allotted to colleges applying for participation, based on one-tenth of the student enrollment as of October 1933. To qualify, the student had to be identified as one who could not continue his studies without aid. Under the program some needy students received tuition, room and board, plus $15 a month allowance.

To lighten financial burdens, some colleges reduced dormitory charges. Nevertheless the dormitories at many schools were virtually empty because living at home became an economic necessity. Students who lived too far from home to commute created associations or cooperatives to bring the cost of living down. One such cooperative, The Dining Association at Cornell, offered 14 meals a week at two dollars. At Texas A & M in 1932, a sociology professor organized twelve students who had no money but were determined to stay in college. They repaired and inhabited an old "haunted house" and then did most of the housework and cooking. By 1933 there were 130 students in ten similar units of cooperative living at Texas A & M. By 1937 cooperatives could be found on more than a hundred campuses, involving over 70,000 students. Co-ops were involved not only in housing but also with book and supply stores, and the organization of inexpensive weekend trips and dances.

Campus activities suffered. Student newspapers lacked income from advertising and circulation. Drama groups had a difficult time selling tickets. Fraternities struggled to find new pledges. To combat the problem of the social pressure for activities that required expenditure of money, the Association of Hoboes was founded on a number of campuses. Members pledged not to spend unnecessarily and were not allowed to borrow. The results were dates consisting of hiking instead of the movies and even of going to the library instead of to town.

The institutions themselves struggled to keep open. Carthage College in Illinois was not the only one that resorted to barter when it accepted coal instead of tuition for a coalminer's daughter. At the University of North Dakota, farm produce was accepted in lieu of tuition. Most institutions had to cut back the size of their faculty, pay their instructors in scrip, or cut salaries by as much as one-third. Students, faculty, and administration were all undeniably in the same boat.

There was, necessarily, a change in the mood on campuses. The *California Daily Bruin* wrote: "Economic necessity has forced thought into the life of the college student. Foolish hazing and traditional exhorbitant, expensive fraternities, excessive drinking and gambling are disappearing. Serious thought on economic and political problems is increasing."

With millions of people unemployed and the all too graphic picture of thousands selling apples on the streets of New York, rummaging through trash cans for food, or standing in line for food or relief, the college student of the Thirties could no longer be the unconcerned creature of the flaming Twenties. Class spirit, so prevalent in the Twenties, was dying. Even at Princeton, some freshmen were no longer wearing the class uniform of black shoes, black socks, corduroy trousers, black jersey, and cap.

To be sure, college days of the Thirties were not like those of the Twenties, but it wasn't just the Depression—although that was undoubtedly the most important factor. Prohibition ended in 1933, and with it ended bathtub gin and insistent drinking that was so much more fun when prohibited than when legal. And by the end of the Thirties, international tension was rising as Hitler moved quickly into the Rhineland. Life was changing, not only on the campuses, but all over.

But it wasn't all grim. The generation of the Thirties managed to find sufficient diversion and fun to release its tensions and divert its anxieties. Playing cards, particularly bridge, was popular. "Monopoly" became a nationwide parlor room fad. The Depression also brought a minor boom in inexpensive sports like bicycling and roller skating.

Radio absorbed college students as well as the rest of the nation. Half-hour variety shows were perfected by Jack Benny, Fred Allen, George Burns and Gracie Allen, Edgar Bergen and Charlie McCarthy. Music reach a peak with Rudy Vallee, Bing Crosby, and Major Bowes. The times brought in "radio dances" particularly at fraternity houses where costs could be cut down to twenty-five cents a couple for a Saturday evening informal dance with radio music, bridge, Ping Pong, and sandwiches and coffee to end the evening. Radio and the emerging popularity of what we now call disc-jockeys made the popular music of the day far more accessible. In fact, it created a new era. In addition to variety shows and music, radio offered shows such as "The Lone Ranger," which began in 1933 and which by 1939 was being heard by 22 million people three times a week. President Roosevelt's "Fireside Chats" reached homes across the country, as well as the Joe Louis boxing matches. Who knows how many coeds called home for reassurance that Martians were not attacking on Sunday, October 30, 1938, when Orson Welles dramatized H. G. Wells's *The War of the Worlds.*

The big music was being made and played by the Big Bands. In 1934 it was Glen Gray and the Casa Loma Orchestra. In 1935 it was Ray Noble, and in 1936 it was Benny Goodman, who had become the High Priest of Swing in fraternities and sororities. Swing tastes, however, differed radically at different campuses. The South liked graceful dance rhythms. Tulane and Newcomb, after a decade of fast dixieland jazz, now preferred the smoother tempo of Whiteman and Lombardo. In the Ivy League, at Yale proms for instance, "Svelte English Tempos of Noble and Amrose" as well as the Dorseys and Benny Goodman were favored.

Even at the depths of the Depression, when attendance at college proms dropped, Big Bands continued to be engaged. In 1937 Rudy Vallee and his trumpeters charged Yale $1,650 and Ozzie Nelson charged Ohio State $1,400. The total cost of taking a girl to a prom varied from school to school: Princeton, $25, Wisconsin, $15, University of California, $10, and Ohio State, $7. At some schools, rather than eliminate the name bands, other forms of economy were instituted to lower the cost. For example, the site of the prom was moved from a downtown hotel to the gymnasium on campus. A more modest decoration budget was established, leaving the Prom Committee with crêpe paper and lots of imagination. Favors were eliminated and it was tacitly agreed not to buy corsages for the girls. By these economies, the cost of a Junior Prom ticket in 1935 at the university of Illinois was cut from $6 to $2.50.

Less affluent schools managed to book the top bands of the period occasionally. By hiring them at cut-rate prices on off nights in the middle of the week when the bands were traveling either to or from Chicago, students at Illinois State Teachers College at Normal could finance their Co-op dances by assessing each student as little as a dollar a year.

Swing and sweet music were the big thing. The leading male vocalist was Rudy Vallee, a Yale man whose hits were peppered with college songs: "My Time Is Your Time," "Life Is Just a Bowl of Cherries," "The Maine Stein Song," "The Whiffenpoof Song," and "I'm Confessing That I Love You." But a new crooner, Bing Crosby, was starting to outpace Vallee with "I Surrender, Dear" and "Sunday, Monday, and Always." Betty Hutton and the jitterbug burst onto the scene. Sweet music included such melodious tunes as "Star Dust," "Night and Day," and "Stormy Weather." The prominent swing bands were those of Benny Goodman, "Count" Basie, Teddy Wilson, Harry James, Artie Shaw, Jimmy and Tommy Dorsey, Bob Crosby, Gene Krupa, Jack Teagarden, Red Norvo, Jimmy Lunceford, Duke Ellington, Glenn Miller, Andy Kirk, Bunny Berigan, and Louis Armstrong. Prior to the Thirties a band was known only by the name of its leader. In the swing period enthusiasts knew the personnel of the leading bands as a baseball fan knows the roster of every major league club. As Irving Kolodin put it, ". . . the rock-ribbed rhythm section of (Count) Basie, (Walter) Page, Jo Jones (drummer), and Fred Green (guitar), is appraised by the experts in terms befitting Connie Mack's Million Dollar Infield of McInniss, Collins, Barry, and 'Home Run' Baker . . ."

Movies were another favorite source of college entertainment in the Thirties, although perhaps only for the more affluent or as a special treat for those without funds. Ronald Coleman, Clark Gable, Gary Cooper, Edward G. Robinson, Gloria Swanson, Katherine Hepburn, Carole Lombard, and Jean Harlow were among the Hollywood stars who took students, at least momentarily, to fantasyland. Lionel Barrymore won an Academy Award for his portrayal in *A Free Soul,* Helen Hayes was named best actress in *The Sin of Madelon Claudet.* Frederic March played the dual roles in *Dr. Jekyll and Mr. Hyde.* Most popular in 1933 were Katherine Hepburn in *Little Women* and Mae West in *She Done Him Wrong. It Happened One Night* and its co-stars Claudette Colbert and Clark Gable walked off with all the top honors in 1934. Bette Davis was chosen the best actress the following year for her role in *Dangerous.* The outstanding films of 1937 included *The Life of Émile Zola, The Good Earth,* and *Captains Courageous.* Mae West commanded the second highest salary in the country in 1937, and Shirley Temple edged upwards to challenge her popularity. In 1938 the top money-maker in films was Walt Disney's *Snow White and the Seven Dwarfs.* Finally in the last year of the decade, Academy Awards were presented to *Gone With the Wind* as the best film and to its star Vivien Leigh as the best actress. The best actor award went to Robert Donat for his portrayal in *Goodbye, Mr. Chips.*

Even if one didn't see the shows on Broadway, one heard tunes on the radio from Jerome Kern's *Roberta* ("Smoke Gets in Your Eyes," "The Touch of Your Hand"); Cole Porter's *Anything Goes* and *Dubarry Was a Lady;* George Gershwin's *Porgy and Bess;* and Rogers and Hart's *On Your Toes.*

College readers found signs of the times in current books

of the Thirties: George Santayana's *The Last Puritan,*
F. Scott Fitzgerald's *Tender Is the Night,* John O'Hara's
Appointment in Samarra, John Steinbeck's *Tortilla Flat*
and *Of Mice and Men,* John Dos Passos's trilogy, *U.S.A.,*
and Ernest Hemingway's *The Fifth Column.* Others, who
were probably more advanced intellectually than their
predecessors in the Twenties, read smuggled copies of D. H.
Lawrence's *Lady Chatterley's Lover* and James Joyce's
Ulysses. Some budding writers tried to blend the style of
Hemingway with the influence of the *New Masses.* But
Dale Carnegie's *How to Win Friends and Influence People*
was the big seller of the mid-Thirties.

Popular culture obviously has a profound effect on
students, sometimes to the great unhappiness of their professors. Princeton's senior class poll in 1935 showed that
Kipling's "If" was the favorite poem of a large majority,
with the *Rubáiyát* and Gray's "Elegy" as the nearest, but
still rather distant, competitors. Noel Coward was regarded
as the supreme dramatist by 135 seniors, while only 107
thought that Shakespeare had the edge on him, and only
79 put Eugene O'Neill above both. Rembrandt lacked one
vote to tie with the magazine artist McClelland Barclay for
the position of supreme painter of all time, and by two-to-
one vote *Anthony Adverse* was judged superior to *Tom
Jones,* behind which *Tale of Two Cities* trailed at no very
great distance.

The Thirties had its share of college hoaxes and pranks,
many of them with a definite political edge. In 1930 two
editors of the Cornell *Sun* made national news when they
sent letters to Republican leaders throughout the country
inviting them to a dinner commemorating the sesqui-
centennial of "Hugo N. Frye, founder of the Republican

Party in New York State." The Vice President of the United States telegraphed in reply, "I congratulate the Republicans on paying this respect to the memory of Hugo N. Frye, and wish you a most successful occasion." The Secretary of Labor proclaimed, "It is a pleasure to testify to the career of that sturdy patriot who first planted the ideals of our party in this region of the country. Were he living today he would be the first to rejoice that our government is still safe in the hands of the people." The Republican leaders were a bit red-faced when the Cornell *Sun* pointed out the phonetic resemblance between Hugo N. Frye and "You Go and Fry!"

At Princeton in 1936 the Veterans of Future Wars was established for the patriotic purpose of collecting their bonuses in advance. Their salute was "hand outstretched, palm up, expectant." Membership spread throughout the undergraduate population of the United States. But the American Legion thought that the Future Veterans were mockers and yellowbellies, aiming to discredit honorable military service. Lewis J. Gorin, founder of the movement, replied, "We merely want our bonus . . . History shows that all bonuses have been paid long after they are due, and we are only asking for ours now."

Several campaigns on national and international issues took place. Reed College (Portland, Oregon) whooped up a campaign to make Wally Simpson Queen of England (Edward abdicated in 1936). Yale seized upon the Supreme Court issue for a Roosevelt-for-King Club, while the Garland School for Home Making (Brookline, Massachusetts) countered with an Eleanor-for-Queen drive.

At the State House in Boston the six-foot Sacred Cod, the emblem of the Commonwealth of Massachusetts, was discovered missing only after a number of telephone calls came in to report the whereabouts of the precious fish in different parts of the state. For days the Boston Police scampered hither and yon in pursuit. On a tip that the fish was in a crate in the basement of an M.I.T. building, the police ripped open a large crate only to find a sardine. Spotting a large silver fish hanging from the weathervane atop the Lowell House tower in Cambridge, policemen climbed up only to discover that it was a silver paper counterfeit . . . The *Harvard Lampoon* offered a large reward. Finally a very surprised policeman found the Sacred Cod of Massachusetts thrown into his arms from a speeding car. The culprits, the *Harvard Lampoon* reported, were never discovered.

In 1937 Princeton attracted national attention with a Lonely Hearts Club. It began with an ad in the Vassar College newspaper: "Hundreds of men are lonely at Princeton. Are you lonely, too? Find your post box lover by writing the Lonely Hearts Club, 121 Little Hall, Princeton, New Jersey. Everything confidential." The authors of this scheme found themselves swamped with 250 letters from 25 different women's colleges and they quickly called a halt, pleading overwork and misunderstanding.

The fad that everyone associates with campus craze, goldfish swallowing, started on March 3, 1939. Lothrop Withington, Jr., accepted a bet by swallowing a live goldfish before an audience that included several Boston newspapermen. As soon as the story hit the papers, the race was on, at first on a small scale. A student at Franklin and Marshall College swallowed three. But the rage took hold, and on a fifty-dollar bet, Irving M. Clark at Harvard swallowed twenty-four, using orange juice as a chaser. He was outdone by one goldfish by a junior at the University of Pennsylvania, and Donald V. Mulcahy of Boston College topped that with twenty-nine.

At this point the Boston Animal Rescue League took

up its cudgels in defense of the goldfish. Boston College issued a warning to its students that no more contests of the goldfish-swallowing type would be tolerated. At Kutztown State Teachers College a student was suspended after swallowing forty-three goldfish in fifty-four minutes for "conduct unbecoming a student in a professional course." The New York *Herald-Tribune* saw fit to remark in an editorial, "If students aren't swallowing goldfish they are up to something else just as foolish—and just as much fun at the moment. That's what keeps students from being dull—and campus life from being a bore. In any event, the goldfish mood will pass. Already news comes from the Middle West that students are eating phonograph records. There is no cause for alarm." One student did actually begin to consume records.

In 1930 women's styles turned back toward the conservative or "normal." The waist came out of hiding, the bosom returned, shoulders squared themselves, and the necklines rose as the hem descended. Socks and saddle shoes were standard campus footgear in the middle Thirties, and blue jeans and beer jackets with shorts appeared by the end of the decade. For wearing to class, the sweater and tweed skirt was standard. Bobbed hair was out, and at the Seven Sisters schools the "in" look was one of "sophisticated simplicity," with the shoulder-length pageboy being particularly popular. One critic of the more casual look complained that "the girls look as if they had dressed in the morning with an eye on the clock and the other on a picture of a new crush on the dresser."

Some Ivy League colleges permitted the luxury of a liberalism virtually unknown west of the Alleghenies: they allowed students to entertain young women visitors privately in their rooms. At Dartmouth students received their "dates" unchaperoned until 11 P.M. To entertain girl visitors until 6 P.M., Yale undergraduates had only to obtain written permission from their deans or the campus police. Official rules at Princeton called for chaperons when undergraduates brought in current flames; however, the regulation had long been ignored.

At Harvard, the "two-women" rule required that the Harvard man had to invite a second girl. The men complained that not only was it difficult to date one attractive girl but that they found it doubly so to get two attractive girls as well as a male companion to entertain the second girl.

Stirred by a Harvard *Crimson* straw vote of twenty-five to one against it and by complaints from house masters, university officials finally threw the unpopular rule out and granted students the right to entertain unchaperoned between 1 P.M. and 7 P.M. attended only by a third person of *unspecified sex*. Girls in nearby Wellesley expressed satisfaction. Asked one: "Why not? It always took two Harvard men to equal one Wellesley girl, according to our mathematics."

The girls at Bennington College in Vermont were unimpressed with the liberalized rules at Harvard. At Bennington, undergraduates could entertain young men in their rooms unchaperoned from noon until supper time, and could sit and chat with them in the luxuriously furnished dormitory drawing-room until 7 A.M. if they so desired. But at most college campuses the strict parietal rules remained.

At coeducational University of Texas, girls were never allowed in the men's rooms. At the University of Chicago, women were barred from male students' rooms at any time, chaperoned or unchaperoned. Stanford University had no specific regulations but observed a carefully honored student code of ethics that banned the entertainment of women in men's chambers. At the University of Wisconsin undergraduates enjoyed the relative liberty of strictly chaperoned "dates" at "approved" lodging houses.

On the campuses, there was less talk about sex. *Fortune Magazine*'s investigation of campus behavior in 1936 reported, "As for sex, it is, of course, still with us. But the campus takes it more casually than it did ten years ago. Sex is no longer news. And the fact that it is no longer news is news." A study by Dunbar Bromley and Florence Haxton Britten based on forty-six colleges and universities showed that half of the college men and a quarter of the college women had had pre-marital sexual intercourse.

Particularly significant was the shift in the girls' attitudes toward marriage. Whereas there was a great deal of feeling in the Twenties that marriage and family life were a mockery, family life became more highly prized as an institution in the Thirties. *Fortune*'s editors said, "Sixty percent of the college girls and fifty percent of the men would like to get married within a year or two of graduation, and fifty percent of each sex would like to have children soon after marriage." But hundreds of thousands of young people who wanted to get married couldn't afford to. The marriage rate per thousand population fell from 10.14 in 1929 to 7.87 in 1932.

Harold Laski in an article in *Harper's Magazine* inquired, "Why Don't Your Young Men Care?" His thesis was that American students refused to be engaged in "politics." "He (the student) studies politics as he studies biology or the fine arts. It is a unit in the taking of a degree. It has no connection with the prospect of citizenship." Professor Laski observed that American students had a hostility to politics and an aversion to public service. The

American student was uninterested and unconcerned about what he could do to improve the social order. In short, he was apathetic. *Outlook* commented on Laski's observations: "It may be so. It was so in our college days . . . in the future, as in the past, America will have to struggle along and solve her problems without the aid of her college students. If political change is necessary, no student bodies will do the voting. If revolution comes, there will be no Harvard or Columbia students on the barricades . . ."

When student ferment did take place in the middle Thirties, it was not within the scope of Laski's definition of "politics," which meant operation within the two-party structure and the formal system of government.

On March 23, 1932, a bus with eighty students from all of the New York colleges as well as from Smith, Cincinnati, Harvard, and Tennessee headed for the Harlan coal regions of Kentucky where a decentralized miners' strike had been taking place. The bus was met in Kentucky by a mob of 200 and the district attorney, who took them to the local court where a judge ordered them to leave Kentucky immediately. Furthermore, to ensure their departure, two attorneys and three armed deputies rode in the bus.

News of the Kentucky trip quickly reached the North. In Chicago, a group of students picketed the home of Samuel Insull for his stake in Kentucky oppression and were arrested by the Chicago police. In Philadelphia a group of students led by an instructor in economics at the University of Pennsylvania carried signs in front of the offices of Drexel and Company, a Morgan affiliate and owners of extensive mining property. They, too, were promptly broken up by the police. James Wechsler observed that the aborted sociological expedition to Kentucky, nevertheless, had an impact. Two similar pilgrimages were attempted at mining areas of Ohio and Illinois.

The important fact was that a greater number of students were becoming aware of some of the evils of the American society.

A student movement was emerging. When Reed Harris, editor of *The Columbia Spectator,* was expelled for publishing a series of articles condemning the operation of the university's dining halls, a mass protest meeting of several thousand students gathered on the steps of Low Library. It was a bold and almost unprecedented move. As one commentator remarked, "Teachers and others familiar with American student life agreed that the Columbia strike was the most militant student demonstration of recent years. It was noted far and wide that at last American college students were becoming excited over something more important than football and crew." The one-day strike at Columbia in April 1932 established the beginning of a student movement and boosted the National Students League (N.S.L.) that organized the strike. The strike was to serve as a model for later events.

Pacifism emerged quite early as a powerful rallying cry of the student movement. Late in 1932, a group of 600 delegates from all over the country gathered at the University of Chicago to develop the guiding principles of the student movement against war. Following the Chicago Congress, two of the students testified in Washington at the House of Representatives against appropriations for R.O.T.C. that were granted to private as well as state universities. Simultaneously in England undergraduates at the Oxford Union voted that "this House will not fight for King and country in any war." The Oxford pledge, as it became known, was immediately picked up in the United States. The *Brown Daily Herald* ran a poll of students to determine their willingness to endorse the Oxford pledge. Other campuses did the same, and the results indicated that undergraduates were overwhelmingly against any war.

At Mount Holyoke the Peace Club took part in many anti-war conferences with the purpose of trying "to educate its members along the lines of peace, and teach them what they, as a group and as individuals, can do to promote world peace." To demonstrate their convictions, 100 girls came to chapel wearing white shirts and sat together to show support of peace.

In 1934 two radical student organizations, the National Student League and the League for Industrial Democracy, planned what became a surprising success—a national student strike against war. Choosing April 13th as the date, because it commemorated the entrance of the United States into the First World War, they called for a one-hour demonstration strike. From 11 A.M. to noon students were to walk out of their classrooms. To everyone's surprise, 25,000 students participated in this nationwide walkout. In the following year, the walkout drew an impressive 175,000 students. Participation came not only from the expected prestige institutions but also from smaller, less visible, institutions. It included from the South, for instance, 1,500 students at Berea, 800 at College of the Ozarks, 100 at Morehouse, and 350 at Louisville. In the Middlewest the list included 500 at Hamline, 100 at Eden, 300 at Drake, 200 at Butler, as well as 3,000 at Minnesota, and 2,000 at Wisconsin. A third walkout in 1936 drew 350,000 participants out of a total college population of one million. At each of these strikes the participants endorsed the Oxford pledge, as revised for American students, to refuse "to support the United States government in any war it may conduct."

The Nation pointed out the changing mood on campus: "Conservatives find it difficult to comprehend that American students are extending their interests beyond football, liquor and sex. Even today the average college man does not read a newspaper regularly but the great interest aroused by the peace campaign augurs well for the future. The American college student may be finally emerging from his mental lethargy."

An anti-R.O.T.C. movement had started. Several students at the University of Maryland, Ohio State, and the University of California refused to participate in compulsory drill and were consequently dismissed. The litigation that resulted upheld the universities. In the case involving the University of California, the U.S. Supreme Court re-enforced the "right" of land-grant colleges to dismiss students who refused to drill. The victory for the state universities and R.O.T.C. was also a victory for the radicals who wanted to push the movement into a more belligerent strategy. Now they had shown that legal and pacifistic means would not work.

What followed was a series of demonstrations on campuses. At the University of Minnesota the young radicals organized "Jingo Day" on the day of the annual R.O.T.C. review. So successful was the demonstration that two weeks later the Board of Regents declared drill optional at the university.

Thus the student movement was involved with the issue of war, as well as concerned with making an alignment with the laboring class.

A group of Yale students tried to assist picketers at the Kirschner Foundry in New Haven. Three M.I.T. students made a tour of inspection to determine the conditions causing industrial tuberculosis at Cambridge Rubber Company. *Progress,* an organ of the "Radical Club" at Oberlin, denounced the "sweat tactics" of the Aluminum Company of America, a company in which the college held four million dollars of stock. Goucher girls supported the pickets at Amalgamated Clothing. Amherst and Smith students raised funds to aid the labor struggle at College Weavers, Inc. Vassar girls aided striking workers at Beacon, New York. And college students in New York City marched on picket lines to aid striking cafeteria workers.

Vassar was the most active of the women's colleges. It had a tradition dating back to "the brave days of Inez Milholland, the pre-War Socialist and suffragette leader of the lush contours and beautiful face who rode white horses in women's rights parades with her hair streaming in the wind." The heroine Mary French in John Dos Passos's *The Big Money,* third volume of the *U.S.A.* trilogy, was a Vassar girl "whose path led to Hull House, to the Pittsburgh steel strikes and to the heart of the Communist movement." Indeed President MacCracken and Ward Dodge in 1934 led Vassar students in a Peace Parade, the National Students Anti-War Week celebration, singing "Baa Baa Bombshell" and "Grandeamus."

The Rutgers Forum had meetings about social issues such as conscription, censorship, and socialism. With the cooperation of such groups as the Liberal Club, the League for Independent Political Action, the Socialist Party chapter, and the League for Industrial Democracy, they brought to the campus speakers such as Communist Earl Browder, Socialist Norman Thomas, Scott Nearing, and Harry Laidler. But "radical" activity at Rutgers was restricted to a very small group and died down by 1938. The majority of students in 1938 were more involved in social matters such as an elective course in Etiquette and Right Living.

At Cornell there was much concern with issues such as the Sacco and Vanzetti trial, striking miners, and military training on campus. In 1936 Senator John J. McNaboe discovered that the American Student Union and the

Young Communist League were on campus and said, "Cornell is a center of revolutionary, communistic activity." President Farrand remained unperturbed, replying that he was not worried about "25 to 30 students with communistic leanings out of a student body of 6,000."

In the early Thirties at Yale, student action was limited to criticizing and reforming the college, not political radicalism. A new student magazine, *Harkness Hoot,* was the main vehicle of expression, and it strongly reflected the language of Mencken. The new journal expressed a general intellectual revolt, but the basic assumptions were anything but proletarian. They were a blend of the old American utopianism with a newer university spirit, for these rebels placed a special trust in the intellect. According to its institutional historian, Yale was very obviously conservative. When accused of "pinkish tendencies," the Yale reaction was flippant. *The News* came out with a statistical "exposé" that 73 percent of undergraduates were sworn Communists. A group of seniors invaded Freshman Commons dressed as the Marx Brothers singing "Marx, Marx on down the field" with signs saying "Everytime we think of Yale we see RED."

In 1934 President Frederick B. Robinson invited the student body of C.C.N.Y. (City College of New York) to a college reception for an official delegation of Italian Fascist students. As the student body hissed the guests, President Robinson reacted with outbursts of "Guttersnipes!" The campus blossomed soon after with lapel buttons reading "I am a Guttersnipe."

Radicalism of the Thirties didn't have an effect on students at all colleges. The student polls at Rhode Island University showed the living figure they most admired in 1930 was Herbert Hoover and in 1933, Jean Harlow. The world's major figure in 1934 was Franklin Delano Roosevelt, with second place given to Maxim Litvinov. By 1937, the polls showed that the world's most important personage was Jesus Christ.

The student movement was not exclusively directed at social issues. There was also concern about questions on the campus itself. At State College of Washington in 1936, the Student Liberty Association organized a strike and printed their demands on a handbill as follows:

1. A progressive clean-minded administration
2. New closing hours: 11:00 weeknights, 1:00 weekends
3. College rules and social rules published
4. No compulsory class attendance
5. Wednesday-night mixers and desserts
6. Abolition of ultra-conservative dictatorial administrative policies.

The sit-down strike was a new idea, taken from the more serious industrial strikes. At Kansas State College, Manhattan, Kansas, journalism students held a sit-down encampment to show the need for a new physical science building. In twelve pup tents, with day and night patrol, they announced they would stay until the Legislature appropriated the money for the building. At Nashville, North Carolina Normal and Teacher's College, there was a sit-down in dorms to demand the dismissal of President Calfee because he had "insulted their pride" by saying, "our students normally subsist at home on a diet of 3 M's, meat, meal and molasses."

Whether the student movement was really producing a new young breed of thinkers and leaders was a subject of debate. *The New Republic* in its January 16, 1935, editorial asked, "Is There a Student Movement in America?" Its answer was:

Certainly there is a great stir and departure from traditional points of view. But our student movement has an elderly quality about it. Its passionless slogans seem to be dictated by old men. Its congresses pass long resolutions about child labor, federal relief, war expenditures, Negro discrimination, but few of the young men and women passing these resolutions seem to know just what sort of good life they want to be allowed to live ... Indeed the student radical who strikes against war is likely to be simultaneously a devoted reader of the *Saturday Evening Post*.

The student movement did not take place without cries of alarm about the strength of Moscow's influence, the perils of Communism, and the threat of socialism. Hearst papers made sure of that. The campus "witch-hunting" and "Red scare" was on by 1935.

William Randolph Hearst tried to Red-bait college professors. The first victim was Professor John Washburne of Syracuse University. Posing as prospective students, Hearst reporters walked into Professor Washburne's office and said they were interested in studying Communism and visiting Russia. The front-page editorial the next day was, "Drive All Radical Professors and Students from University." Dr. Washburne was quoted as admitting that he was a Communist. Hearst reporters were ordered to run a series of such exposés of radical professors. The same stunt was tried at Columbia, but the professor found out who the "students" were and prevented an incident. Outraged by this attempted frameup, professors from Columbia, N.Y.U., and Union Theological Seminary asked the Congressional Committee on Un-American Activities to investigate Hearst's "campaign of terrorism against teachers in American colleges." The appeal was ignored.

Charles Walgreen, owner of the drugstore chain, assisted Mr. Hearst in getting a legislative committee to investigate the University of Chicago where, Mr. Walgreen contended, his niece had been required to read the *Communist Manifesto* and exposed to ideas of free love. Similar witch-hunts were taking place throughout the country. On the student front, vigilantism was growing on the Right. A cleavage was developing on the campuses between the Right and the Left, but it didn't last long, because the tactics of the movement were shifting. Hal Draper identifies this shift as the second period of the movement:

> But the second period of the student movement was now beginning, in which the highly ideological leadership of the Communist students made a turn toward "de-ideologizing" and depoliticalizing the movement in line with their new orientation. The "non-ideological" mask that was to be adopted was incompatible even with ideology in a liberal form. What was beginning was the cant of speaking in the name of "The Students" whose aspirations and most secret thoughts always somehow coincided with the latest pronouncements of the YCL (Young Communist League) . . .

Draper identifies the last chapter as occurring after September 1939. After four years of the student anti-war movement, the Second World War was inaugurated with the Hitler-Stalin Pact. Communist power was now an ally of Hitler, especially in the eyes of Jewish students, and many left the movement.

Murray Kempton estimates that, at the very most, 15,000 persons were members of the left-wing organizations on campus during the Thirties. The American Student Union (ASU) at its peak had only 12,000 members. The Young Communist League had fewer than 5,000 at any one time. Toward the latter part of the Thirties, the Young People's Socialist League had fewer than a 1,000 members and the Young Trotskyites had fewer than 500.

Murray Kempton reminisced about this:

So much of the tumult was manufactured then, as detached from commitment in its way as the laughter was. The stage itself held very few people and most of those are gone. The tumult is gone, too, and the laughter, because no one seems to exercise the detachment of laughter about such matters any longer. Most persons who are articulate about that lost time treat it as seriously as only a very few of us did when we thought it had reality so very long ago.

So many of us are gone now, gone without trace, this bright young legion of the elect who were supposed to be the leaders of their generation and the beacon for its future. The American Student Union was at its zenith in 1937. Its pronouncements were taken seriously by adults, even the sort of adults whose custom it is not to bear fools gladly. It was discussed as a serious menace by the Hearst papers; and it set the tone of antimilitarist, antifascist fever which many of its friends and enemies alike universalized as the mood of the college undergraduate in the mid-Thirties.

Joseph Wood Krutch wrote in *The Nation* that on the campuses he visited he found "no new spirit abroad, no changed attitude assumed toward a much-changed world. Out of a student body of a thousand there may be eight Socialists or Communists where there were five before . . . They are not rebellious, or cynical, or even melancholy. They do what they are told, believe what they are told, and hope for the best."

At a state teachers' college in Missouri, Krutch interviewed a student who represented what he thought was such a minority point of view. In answer to the question of what the students thought, the interviewee replied, "I can only tell you . . . what they *ought* to think. They ought to think that their teachers and their parents have let them down. Look at me, for instance, I have been going to school

all my life and I have always been told the same thing.
'Get an education. The world has need for you and you
must be prepared. Stick to your books, learn your profession, and we will do the rest. The world is crying for
trained men and it is waiting for you to assume the responsibilities which you must expect.' I was a good boy and I
stuck to my books. I prepared myself diligently for the task
I was going to be called upon to perform. The only fear I
had was the fear of not being good enough. But where is
that task and what has happened? Nobody knows what to
do with me or the education I was so careful to get. I am
not bitter. I believe that ultimately something can be done
about it, and I wouldn't be a member of the Socialist Party
if I didn't. But I do feel that I have been let down. I was
urged to prepare myself for a busy world and I find that I
have only prepared myself for a vacuum instead. No, most
students don't feel that way. They don't feel any way at all."

Many of the assumptions of the American people were
being shaken. The assumption before the Depression had
been that a college education would guarantee success.
Parents with marginal means who managed to get their
sons into prestigious colleges to give them "advantages"
believed that it is not what you know but who you know.
There had been a general assumption, particularly in the
Twenties, that there was no end to the growth of the
American economy and that hard work and ambition
would bring personal success. Failure was only for those who
were incompetent. Probably for the first time in American
higher education, the college student feared for his future
even though supposedly well armed with his diploma.

The editors of *Fortune* in 1936, speaking of the majority
of college students, wrote:

The present-day college generation is fatalistic . . . the inves-
tigator is struck by the dominant and pervasive color of a gener-

ation that will not stick its neck out. It keeps its shirt on, its pants buttoned, its chin up, and its mouth shut. If we take the mean average to be the truth, it is a cautious, subdued, unadventurous generation, unwilling to storm heaven, afraid to make a fool of itself, unable to dramatize its predicament... Security is the summum bonum of the present college generation.

Yet the influence of the minority who did stick their necks out should not be underestimated because of the early demise of their organizations. As Hal Draper comments:

The student movement was one of the first casualties of the Second World War, but its impact was not ended. For the next couple of decades at least, wherever anything was stirring in the labor movement or in liberal campaigns, wherever there was action for progressive causes or voices were raised in dissent from the Establishment, there one was sure to find alumni of this student movement, who had gotten their political education and organizational training and experience in the American Student Union or the Student League for Industrial Democracy or the National Student League. . . .

CHAPTER IV

G.I.s ON CAMPUS: THE FORTIES

Following Pearl Harbor on December 7, 1941, and the United States entry into World War II, college men were determined, ready to go, and waiting for orders. As late as the fall of 1942, no clear or consistent policy had emerged concerning the role of the country's colleges and universities in the war effort. President Roosevelt had told college men that it was their "patriotic duty" to stay at their studies until drafted, so that they would be prepared "for greatest usefulness to their country." So, many waited for the draft call and in the meantime continued in college not knowing when their education would be interrupted. But many college men suffered from deeply troubled consciences, especially as neighbors and friends enlisted or were drafted. To speed up the production of college-educated talent, colleges geared up to a year-round basis, to permit the completion of the baccalaureate in three years or less.

Before the storm of World War II broke, a Gallup Poll found moviegoers strongly antipathetic toward war pictures, but *Gone With the Wind,* launched in late 1939, had overwhelming appeal in its Civil War scenes. Once in the war, the temper of students and other young Americans reversed. *Sergeant York* (a World War I hero) in 1941, *Mrs. Miniver* (the English housewife heroine) in 1942, and *Lifeboat* (with Tallulah Bankhead) were followed by a spate of war documentaries. *Stalingrad* was the most unforgettable. Comedies featured Bob Hope, of course; musicals turned martial (*This Is the Army*) and finally, in 1946, came the classic *The Best Years of Our Lives*. Probably no American war movie could match the artistry of Rosellini's *Open City*, about Rome.

Churchill's *Blood, Sweat and Tears* was a best seller at the beginning of the war, with *The Grapes of Wrath* (1939) and *For Whom the Bell Tolls* (1940) still going strong. *See Here, Private Hargrove* (1942) sold two and a half million copies in four years, and Bill Mauldin created Sad Sack, the private.

The war revved up sentimental spirits with "This Is the Army, Mr. Jones," "When the Lights Go On Again," and (especially Frank Sinatra's rendition) "I'll Be Seeing You." The German song "Lili Marlene" was adopted by all the armies, and Marlene Dietrich made it her own.

College life necessarily changed. At Cornell, house parties and the traditional Junior Week activities were canceled. At Wisconsin even Rush Week for the sororities was dampened. The parties were much simpler. Gone were the orchestras and expensive teas. As one girl said, "It doesn't seem right to be spending a lot of money, so we buy war bonds instead... But its not those little things that make the difference. It's the whole atmosphere, and not knowing what's going to happen." On the other hand, another kind of phenomenon was taking place at some normally party-loving campuses. Whereas a sorority girl was expected to wait until her junior year to go steady, her senior year to get engaged, and graduation to get married, the number of marriages and engagements tripled in the spring of 1942.

Over 90 percent of U.C.L.A.'s fraternity men signed up for active service. But at Princeton, which had sent 92 percent of its seniors to the armed services in 1917, only 6 percent of the seniors had enlisted in 1942. Following the announced governmental policy that education is a national resource of first importance, the emphasis was put on speeding up the curriculum rather than scrapping it.

Subject matter important to the war effort was soon offered at the colleges. The Engineering, Science, and Management War Training (E.S.M.W.T.) program administered by the U.S. Office of Education was offered at 190 colleges and universities to provide short, college-level training courses in technical subjects for war-industry workers. Intensive language courses in Russian, Arabic, Chinese, Japanese, Hindustani, Swahili, Malay, Mongolian, Persian, Thai, and Turkish were offered at a handful of universities. Almost every college and university, including the women's, added new special "war" courses to its curriculum: communications, map reading, military history, ballistics, and the American heritage, among others.

Some 300 institutions participated in the two major college training programs: the Army Specialized Training Program (A.S.T.P.) and the Naval College Training Program (V-12). In these programs the men were on active duty, in uniform, receiving pay, and under general military discipline. The trainees carried heavy work loads. For instance, under A.S.T.P. the trainees had approximately 59 hours of supervised activity a week as follows: 24 hours (minimum) classroom and laboratory work, 24 hours required study, 5 hours military instruction, and 6 hours physical instruction. At many campuses the government contracted for services and space in the training of men.

At the University of Chicago over 3,000 uniformed soldiers and sailors took over two gymnasiums as dormitories and other buildings for classrooms.

As reported by Raymond Walters in the fall of 1943, the number of full-time civilian students had dropped by 38 percent as compared to the enrollment of the previous year. Filling up some of the empty seats were approximately 288,000 military students at about 420 institutions. Some graduate schools dropped in enrollments by as much as 60 percent and only a handful of students were in law schools.

An interesting effect of the war upon collegiate attendance was the phenomenal increase in enrollment of women. As Barnard's Dean Virginia Gildersleeve explained it, "The Government has the boys. Families have college money for the girls." Raymond Walters adds a second explanation that it was "the conviction of many young women that it is up to them to keep burning the light of liberal education in this dark war period." Of 95 women's colleges, 59 reported increases of 5 to 35 percent in 1943. By 1944 the University of Wisconsin had nine freshman girls to one freshman boy and at Ohio State University the ratio was four girls to one boy.

College days during the war years were certainly not normal, but no one had anticipated how very different the post-war period would become on the campuses.

Journalists were calling 1946 "The Year of Frenzy," "The Year of Bullbat," "The Year of Frustration." From the beginning of the U.S. involvement in World War II until the end of the war, normal college life had been practically nonexistent.

The G.I. Bill of Rights gave the World War II veteran,

among other things, an opportunity to go to college. In the fall of 1946, the total enrollment at American colleges was 57 percent higher than the figures of 1939. Veterans comprised 57 percent of the total full-time enrollment and 78 percent of the male students at the large universities.

College days on the American campuses would never be the same again. Higher education was democratized. Opportunities for college and graduate school were given to hundreds of thousands who otherwise would not have gone. There was a shortage of classroom space, college teachers, and books. But no shortage had quite the impact that the shortage of dormitory accommodations did.

College days for the returning G.I. from 1945 to 1950, particularly for those who were married, are remembered more for the housing and living conditions than for anything else. In the fall of 1946, the half-filled universities and colleges were suddenly bulging with veterans, their wives, and their children. For the married G.I. the selection of the college of his choice was sometimes influenced by where his family could stay rather than the scholastic standing of the institution. Most colleges responded as generously as they could. Some grudgingly made emergency provisions. Others were blunt: You are admitted to our school, but please leave your wife and children at home. For many, these were grim times and few thought that they would ever look back at them nostalgically.

Portable dorms mushroomed on the campuses in the form of Quonset huts, trailers, prefabricated houses, and hastily converted barracks. At the University of Chicago, 45 Army barracks were thrown up on Dudley Field, with eight families to each—four upstairs and four downstairs. One ex-G.I. student, now a college vice president, remembers that the entire "apartment" included two bedrooms in a space so confined that the Salvation Army vacuum cleaner with no extension could clean the whole place while attached to the kitchen outlet.

At Rhode Island State, 28 Quonset huts were jammed on Vet Row with eleven students to a hut. Wisconsin had 1,866 veterans in a powder plant 35 miles from the campus and 1,660 more at an Army airfield. Boarding houses and fraternity houses were converted into family apartments. Double- and triple-decker bunks were installed in dormitories. Some couples were forced to stay at hotels at day rates until quarters could be found. At Michigan State, beds had to be moved on and off the gymnasium floor according to the basketball schedule. University of Maine students moved into converted poultry houses. At the University of Southern California two students lived in an automobile for seven months and studied at night under street lamps. But it would take a good story to one-up the three students who lived in the basement of a funeral parlor.

The shortage of bathrooms, running water, heat, and even lighting was only part of hazards of the time. Running water in a trailer was a large tin can over the sink with a spigot and a pail underneath the sink. Some trailer camps were furnished with outdoor "johns" and communal bath centers. The vet studied at a two-foot-square desk. The great ambition for these couples was to move up the ladder to the next level of gracious living, the tar-paper shacks equipped with kerosene stoves and ice boxes—and we don't mean refrigerators.

The monthly living allowance under the G.I. Bill for married veterans was $90 a month in 1945 and the sum was raised twice: to $105 and later to $120. Many couples paid between $40 and $50 per month for rent and it was virtually impossible to live on the balance. For some, there was parental help. Some were lucky enough to have savings. Those who bought a War Bond each month in the service were now cashing a War Bond each month. Odd jobs were not easy to come by in college towns, but the veterans and their brides raised funds however they could. Four times a year, one could sell a pint of blood for ten dollars.

The couple that got the Fuller Brush franchise for the neighborhood was wealthy by comparison, though sales were made by bike. (No cars, new or old, were available on most campuses in 1946 and 1947.) One such couple had enough money left over to tour Europe by bike, with their three-year-old in back. Few of the wives worked— they had two or three small children. One spouse of a medical student, not as young as the others, cared for six children in a barracks apartment and at night worked in a bakery.

Above all, the G.I. was determined to finish his education. Having just put up with the discomforts imposed upon him by military life, he was willing to put up with it for a little while longer.

Thousands of babies were born to student-veterans living on campus. In 1946 Cornell reported that it already had more than 500 children on campus, Indiana University was anticipating 400 new babies, while the University of Illinois looked forward to a substantial increase in the 800 they already had.

For many, government payments were inadequate for rising health and living costs. Infirmary and medical care at the university was not normally extended to wives and children. Lack of play space for small children was a general complaint, and lost children were an everyday occurrence. One boy toddler from a barracks was found asleep under a sofa on the third floor of the women's dormitory after an all-day search by students, faculty, and campus caretakers. Often, as at Chicago, student parents formed and staffed their own nursery schools.

One of the most irksome problems was that of laundry, particularly for families living in trailers and temporary houses where only community washtubs were available. Sterilizing baby bottles and making formula were doubly difficult without easy access to running hot water or dependable stoves. And as for diapers, only the financially elite had service.

Mrs. G.I. as a newlywed had to learn how to cook under the worst circumstances. She had an impossibly tight budget and kitchen. She learned to make casseroles of every shape and form on the kerosene stoves. She collected and traded hundreds of recipes for hamburger, frankfurters, Velveeta cheese, Cornflakes, and chicken. They entertained other G.I. couples with spaghetti and Chianti. Somehow or other, they ate. One mother today puts it bluntly: "There were no seconds at our table."

Many G.I. student families formed buying co-ops, and meeting the truck delivering canned goods at the Quonset or barracks grounds one day a week was tantamount to meeting the stagecoach in pioneer days. They planted their own vegetable gardens anywhere they could find land, to harvest during the summer session. As married G.I.s were eager to finish schooling as soon as they could, many colleges arranged summer courses as well as permitting heavier schedules for more credits. Eager beavers could even sometimes complete four years in two and a half.

For those couples who did manage to find an apartment, the next difficult task was to find furniture. In 1946, American industry was not yet geared to the post-war economy. Materials were still short, and appliances such as refrigerators and stoves were scarce and expensive. It was difficult enough to buy a bed or a crib, much less a sofa or dining room table. Card tables borrowed from relatives and friends served as dining room tables as well as desks.

Painted or covered orange crates made good bookcases, end tables, and bureaus, as in the days of the Depression campus. Lamps were made out of bottles and jugs, or anything with a suitable shape.

But not everyone had it so rough. At Hamilton College, a men's college in upstate New York, one of the dormitories, Carnegie Hall, was converted for use by married couples and their children. Not only were they bringing up babies in a men's dormitory, but in a reckless moment, the administration allowed them to have pets. Special privileges were given to the wives to attend classes, and to use the library, piano practice rooms, tennis courts, golf links, and skating rinks. Once a week they had exclusive use of the gymnasium and swimming pool. As for sunbathing, the president was quoted as saying, "Any place on the campus is all right, but there's a nice patch of grass right back of my office."

Mrs. G.I. had frequently finished college and was now making sacrifices to get her husband through college. There was a unity of purpose and a common goal. Mr. G.I. was out to get the required credits with as good grades as possible as quickly as possible. The bread-and-butter motive activated him. It was grim for many. And yet, there was a kind of camaraderie and spirit among the married couples that probably has never been duplicated since on the American campus. The sense of cooperation, common purpose, and friendship was far greater than that between sorority sisters. Mrs. G.I. could always count on her neighbor to babysit. They invited one another to dinner several times a week when the men didn't have to study. Or the girls would plan evening bridge sessions so that their husbands would be free to work. They had "bring your own" parties; the hostess provided only potato chips and glasses to celebrate the end of exam periods. A collection among the occupants of the trailer camp was almost always successful in pulling a couple out of a crisis or misfortune.

At Michigan State the young married women organized themselves into "Spartan Wives." By 1947, they were publishing their own newspaper, had their own radio program, gave swimming, riding, and craft classes, and ran pot-luck suppers, bridge tournaments, and song fests.

With the end of the war, the big bands had died, and the campuses saw no more of them. The singers who had been featured with them emerged in a new glory—Frank Sinatra, Dinah Shore, and Perry Como. But at colleges, it was the folksingers who appeared. John Lomax had established the Archives of American Folksongs in the Library of Congress. Leadbelly, Burl Ives, Woody Guthrie, Pete Seeger, Josh White, and the Almanac Singers sang campus concerts for G.I. students in bluejeans and their wives in dresses with the New Look length.

Combos came in to replace the big bands at dances, and for more conventional students the songs they had known before the war came back, and their record sales soared— "Peg-O-My-Heart," "Near You," "Tea for Two" (with Sinatra and Dinah Shore). In 1949, the best-selling records were Buddy Clark with "Ballerina," Perry Como with "Haunted Heart," Ella Fitzgerald with "Lady Be Good," and Sinatra (again) with "I've Got a Crush on You." Old-fashioned romance had survived the war.

The unmarried veteran returning to college after an interruption of three or four years had a decisive effect on campus. Older, more mature, and more serious, he didn't have much time for traditional extracurricular activities, even if he was single. He often considered the coed on campus childish and silly. For her part, the coed complained that the veterans were too serious and unfriendly. Whether married or not, the G.I. was often characterized as a

D.A.R. (Damned Average Raiser). A study of academic achievement at Cornell University showed the highest grades were achieved by veterans with children, the next by married veterans, then by unmarried veterans, and finally, at the bottom of academic ladder was the non-veteran student.

Whether or not such a study would be generally true, there was no doubt that veterans were more serious than the usual students. When a coal strike threatened to close classes at one college, a veteran wrote in the school paper, "There's no reason why classes can't keep going coal or no coal. A lecture sounds just as good whether the speaker is wearing an overcoat or a sport shirt." At one of the big football campuses, G.I. pressure ended the long tradition of canceled Monday-morning classes after big football weekends.

At the University of Rhode Island, the Junior Prom and the whole constellation of extracurricular delights were revived in the late Forties. The observation was made, however, that "while they formed an important part of campus life, they no longer formed the core." On the other hand, Rutgers's institutional historian reported that athletics during the post-war period achieved a "Golden Age" because of the mature, well conditioned, and enthusiastic ex-soldiers.

The student-veteran had high expectations of the standards of academic life and, at times, he was critical of their shortcomings. Historian Sidney A. Burrell wrote:

Like most young persons who have lived through long periods of confrontation with personal danger and doubtful future, the postwar student veterans were not notably reverent toward the academic *status quo*. At times, in fact, they were less than kind. Eminent faculty who had lectured in arcane fashion for years often found themselves challenged for lack of clarity in presentation, for repetitious dullness, for failure to keep abreast of the latest scholarship that their auditors sometimes knew far better than they. The discontent could be very vocal. One distinguished professor whose classes I attended was told by a delegation of students that his lectures were badly organized, difficult to follow, and impossible to take notes on. The critics were right too. In another instance, sharp classroom rejoinder very nearly reduced a young instructor to tears. The student veteran hated cant, wanted to understand what he heard, and fully expected his instructors to have things thought out carefully before stepping into a lecture room.

There was, of course, some discontent from those who wanted to preserve the traditions of Joe College. Veterans refused to wear freshmen beanies or be subjected to hazing. College class distinctions, in any case, were mixed up by veterans returning from various classes. Those who joined fraternities helped to bring about changes not only in hazing practices but also in the rituals and discriminatory clauses. At the fraternities the vets often refused to take part in some parts of "Hell Week" or hazing practices. At the University of Washington, twelve pledges—all vets— walked out after hazing started. "No 18-year old kids are going to warm our bottoms." At Northeastern University a sophomore "active" ordered a pledge to light his cigarette for him. The pledge, an ex-Major in the Air Force, gave the sophomore heated and explicit instructions about how he could dispose of the pledge pin.

Nor were prospective fraternity men likely to put up with the religious and racial barriers to membership. Many of those who had gone through a war beside Jews, Negroes, and men of other backgrounds were unwilling to tolerate such discrimination in all its blatant organizational forms. Even Hollywood discovered discrimination and issued war films in which the heroes were victims of racial injustice.

The general issue rose in the late Forties, but because it came to a head in the Fifties, it is described in the next chapter.

John Hersey's paeon to a war hero, *A Bell for Adano* (1945), probably never appealed to the college intellectual, but Norman Mailer's *The Naked and the Dead* brought World War II back to reality, soon to be followed by another stark modern masterpiece, Hersey's *Hiroshima*.

In the mid-1940s, while America underwent its realization of war as war, a French literary revolution was under way, the impact of which would not reach the American campus for almost a decade. The existentialists Jean Paul Sartre and Albert Camus launched a new philosophy of disillusionment. The two top best sellers of 1946 were, strangely, *The Snake Pit* and *Peace of Mind*. The American literary decade closed with the new post-war world examined in Arthur Miller's *Death of a Salesman*, George Orwell's *1984*, and T. S. Eliot's *The Cocktail Party*.

The Second Sex by Simone de Beauvoir reflected the emerging turmoil of the free woman. Jackson Pollock dripped his first painting, a mere suggestion of the shattering visions to come. Alexander Calder and Henry Moore began the ironworks mode of sculpture that would take ten years to gain general acceptance. And the first hilly roof of prefabricated concrete was invented—an innovation that would influence the new buildings on many campuses, marking a complete and daring contrast to the halls of ivy.

But the class of 1949 was indeed different from any college class before or after. It was the class that really established the gray flannel mentality that was to dominate the Fifties. At the time of graduation in June 1949, the average male senior was twenty-four years old. Of the male graduates 70 percent were veterans and 30 percent were married. As *Fortune Magazine* reported, "the Class of

'49 was 'the soberest, most trained graduating class in U.S. history.' " It was a class that was eager to make itself useful to business. It looked to big business for security, and it was a cautious generation that turned its back on venture. Above everything security was the great goal; they didn't want risks. They seemed haunted by the fear of a recession.

In the colleges canvassed by *Fortune,* only 2 percent of the seniors had any intention of going into business for themselves. Furthermore, many seniors stayed away from jobs that were highly pressured and that demanded an entrepreneurial spirit. If 1949 had a class bogey, it was ulcers. It was the floor, not the ceiling, that the men of 1949 were concerned about.

This was a practical, job-oriented class. Whereas 27 percent of the students in 1929 majored in the humanities, only 10 percent of this class did so. Many G.I.s looking ahead to greater job security went on to graduate school, taking full advantage of the G.I. Bill while they could.

The class of 1949 was a settling-down generation. The Depression and the war gave them a preoccupation with security. Although many had predicted that veterans would be impatient with authority, the effect of military life caused quite the opposite. The veteran was not afraid of bigness, he had learned how to keep his nose clean, and how to live in an organization where conformity was emphasized and reward de-emphasized. There was safety in numbers.

The Good Life meant: a good wife, a comfortable house, about three children, one, perhaps two cars, and later, with luck, a summer cottage. There was little speculation about how much money they might make twenty or thirty years hence, but generally they didn't think of anything over $10,000—ever.

Fortune Magazine summed up what the class of 1949 meant by security:

> Spiritually, it means working for people in the sense of service, of justifying one's place in the community. Materially, it is, simply, working *under* them. The class of '49 wants to work for somebody else—preferably someone big. "I never saw a bunch that so wanted to make this free-enterprise system work," says a professor of business administration, "but they are interested in the system rather than the individual enterprise. They will be technicians—not owners."

The students of the Forties became the parents of the college students of the late Sixties. Should it be surprising to find a generation gap?

CHAPTER V

THE SILENT GENERATION

THE college students of the Fifties have been called the "found," the "baffling," or "transitional" generation. Fred Hechinger of *The New York Times* dubbed this period of looking inward as "privatism." But the "Silent Generation" seems to have stuck.

The "silence" of this generation stemmed mainly from its lack of commitment or forcefulness in political affairs. In terms of decibel levels, these college students made their share of noise with panty raids and other pranks, although there was some concern that Joe College was dying. But this generation didn't really rock the boat in any dramatic way. At that time, neither did anyone else.

America entered the second half of the twentieth century without any great fanfare or euphoria. Harry S Truman was still President, with post-war problems of inflation, strikes, and the emergence of the Cold War. G.I.s who had so dominated the campus scene after the war were graduating. Such a period might have been a return to "normalcy," but it wasn't. The decade following the Second World War was by no means the same as that which followed the First.

Before 1950 ended, the North Koreans had crossed the 38th Parallel and American soldiers were again drawn into battle, this time under the banner of the United Nations.

The fighting didn't evoke the patriotic fervor that characterized the Second World War, but neither was the conflict rejected or demonstrated against as was the war in Vietnam in the late Sixties. The Silent Generation took all things in stride—or philosophically, if you will. Reserve units were called up to defend South Korea. Draft calls were increased. No great outcry came from the campuses against war. They went if they were drafted, and if they weren't, they were glad to be left alone. Some joined the R.O.T.C. and others joined reserve units to put off the draft until after college or to a more convenient time. "Maybe it'll be all over by then," was the hope. Many took the deferment examinations that would exempt them from the draft. For those who went there was the Korean G.I. Bill of Rights to look forward to.

The Korean War was disruptive but engendered no great emotions, antagonism, or enthusiasm among those in college. It turned into a different kind of war, a limited one in which there could be no victory. General Douglas MacArthur was fired on April 11, 1951 by President Truman, and the General gave his "old soldiers never die" speech to Congress when he returned. General Eisenhower took a leave of absence from the Presidency of Columbia University to become supreme commander of the Western European defense forces, the North Atlantic Council. He returned in 1952 to run for the Presidency of the United States. The Korean Armistice was signed on July 27, 1953. U.S. Armed Forces casualties in Korea totaled 137,501, of which 25,604 were killed, 103,492 were wounded, and 7,955 were reported missing. The Cold War then dominated international affairs. John Foster Dulles's strategy was summed up as "brinkmanship."

Who knows what creates a mood of any decade? One can argue that the Silent Generation merely reflected the mood of the nation: tired of war, afraid of inflation, and frightened by an internal Communist conspiracy. William H. Whyte, Jr., in *The Organization Man,* pictured college as a training camp for the type:

He—the student of the Fifties—wore gray flannel suits, supposedly, dressed in tie and jacket, saw no evil, spoke no evil, and heard no evil. He worked hard at his studies— grant him at least that—for he was determined to "make it." In a period of economic boom, he was to move up the corporate ladder cooperating with all those that he had to cooperate with. He was to make no waves. He plodded along—building America's economy.

She—the coed of the Fifties—was glad to have men back on the campus. But she wasn't the feminist of earlier eras. She, the college woman of the Fifties, wanted no career. She wanted a husband, children, and a house in the suburbs. And she wanted it right after graduation.

They—the young couple of the Fifties—didn't want to work up to the suburbs. They wanted it now. The whole bit—the house, two cars, dishwasher, children, P.T.A., and security.

Who was to blame them? Born of parents of the Depression, brought up during the Second World War, and now in college by the grace of God and a booming economy—they were pragmatic and sober. They had, by the accident of having been born when they were, missed the Depression as far as their memory went. They missed the World War also because they were too young, and now they were in college. They were there while the H-bomb was being improved in efficiency and perhaps in "cleanliness." The future, when it didn't look hopeful and attractive, was fatalistically to be consumed by The Bomb. If not, then they had better make the best of it—and so they did.

What was there to stir this generation? Truman wasn't very inspiring to them and Ike for all his virtues did not bring innovations or creativity. Adlai Stevenson tried to stir young people but he could reach only some of them. Witty, urbane, and sophisticated, Stevenson lost the Presidential race against Eisenhower. By the end of the campaign of 1952, "eggheads" were out.

Post-war collegiate sports, which might have been started up again, were devastated by the gambling scandals erupting in 1951 at Madison Square Garden in New York City with C.C.N.Y. and N.Y.U. basketball teams. The cribbing scandal at West Point didn't help.

Having graduated most of the returning G.I.s, who had in some minds ruined Joe College, fraternities tried to turn back the clock and couldn't. The 1954 Supreme Court decision on racial segregation had a message for Sigma Chi and other such "Aryan" fraternities. Fraternities on the local level agonized over whether they should try to "buck" the national organization by pledging students of minority groups. Yale seniors kept vacillating about whether to continue "Tap."

Values were changing in the Fifties. Ivy League colleges were beginning to recruit at public high schools in order to look for academic talent rather than merely proper upbringing. Fraternities were being integrated—slowly and quietly. For professors whose last "normal" class was that of 1940, this class of the Fifties was a much more serious and intelligent generation of students. American higher education was reaching a far wider segment of the population; the G.I. Bill had broken the barrier. College was no longer only for the elite. Universities, particularly state institutions that could not delimit their student bodies, expanded and enlarged. Parents of all economic levels were sending their children to college, with or without the G.I. Bill.

The decade presented decided alternatives for collegians to ponder or act upon. The first contraceptive pill appeared in 1952, the year of the hydrogen bomb. Hollywood was being cleansed of Communism while it offered such sex symbols at Rita Hayworth, Marilyn Monroe, and Marlon Brando. Arthur Miller wrote *The Crucible,* a tragedy about the Salem witch-hunts, to reflect upon those of the Un-American Activities Committee and the rumbling Senator Joseph McCarthy. Tennessee Williams brought to the footlights the submerged subject of homosexuality. And book readers were stirred by the new role of the very young girl as she appeared in the famous and contrasting books *The Diary of Anne Frank* (1952), *Bonjour Tristesse* (1955), and *Lolita* (1958). The word coed disappeared on many campuses. Girl students became students, without special designation.

But something was missing in this generation. There was no spirit, no élan. The academic motto for 1953 was: "Don't say, don't write, don't join," as Senators McCarthy and Jenner and Congressman Velde began to investigate Communism at colleges and universities. Students were afraid to sign petitions or join political organizations. One professor said, "When I was an undergraduate 35 years ago I enjoyed one luxury students don't have now—the luxury of making a mistake."

The Congressional investigations delved into the past of professors to see with whom they associated in college, what organizations they had joined, what they wrote that could be considered un-American. Students saw what could be dredged up from college days and used as incriminating evidence years later. So they were cautious not to fall into similar traps. Even established professors on the campuses began to watch what they wrote, said in private, or even lectured. It was commonly known on some campuses that certain students were reporting to the F.B.I. on statements made by professors. Thus many students were also fearful about being outspoken. Writings were rechecked carefully for sentences that might conceivably be twisted around to trap the author. The Attorney General's List, as it was popularly known, contained the names of organizations considered to be Communist, fascist, or infiltrated. That many people belonged to some of the groups meant nothing, though outstanding members of the government had at some period belonged to some of them. It was a checklist used by college administrators to avoid hiring professors who might prove embarrassing to the school. Teachers and students were well aware of this widely circulated list.

In June 1953 the State Department revealed that overseas libraries of the U.S. Information Service had been burning books that could prove embarrassing in Congressional investigations. The first year of the flying saucers, 1955, was McCarthy's peak. Terror was in the air. Even Hubert Humphrey, progressive leader of the Democrats in the Senate, had introduced the bill in the Senate that outlawed the Communists (though other laws gave full protection against subversion), probably as protective coloring for the coming elections in which McCarthy played a prominent part.

With this caution, if not fear, on the part of professors, it was not surprising that students of the Fifties became reluctant to take part in political discussion, join organizations, or sign petitions. A pall was cast on the campuses, creating doubt as to how far scholars and students should go in discussing controversial issues. An atmosphere of general mistrust existed. One student of the period recalls that in his course in Contemporary Civilization, the professor ruefully pointed to the syllabus reading list, which contained the *Communist Manifesto*. With a grim smile he said, "Go home, pull down the blinds and read it." The same student remembers that a man on the street soliciting signatures on his clipboard for a Geneva peace conference was shunned by all students who passed him.

After the first several months of investigations, Senator William Jenner and his subcommittee reported that of the more than 100 witnesses who had appeared before the committee, 82 pleaded the Fifth Amendment and refused to say whether or not they had ever been members of the Communist Party. Three admitted membership in the Communist Party at one time but refused "to supply further details." A typical case was that of Robert Gorham Davis. He had joined the Communist Party in the middle Thirties while teaching at Harvard; two years later, disillusioned by the Nazi-Soviet pact, he quit.

The effect of the investigations was to force colleges and universities to take a stand on each of the witnesses that appeared before the Congressional committees. But students, by and large, did not take any public stands to defend their professors in the early and middle Fifties. They watched in horror, but they watched cautiously. It wasn't until the late Fifties that they began to get involved. As one undergraduate of the period recalled, "The university suffered generally from a clobbered feeling. The apathy came down from above. As somebody said of the faculty and students of those days, "It was a case of the bland leading the bland.' "

While all institutions appeared to agree that they didn't want Communists on their faculties, a decision had to be made as to whether past membership would affect their status or the more difficult question of whether a faculty member should be fired for refusing to answer Congressional investigators on the grounds that his answers might incriminate him. President Nathan Pusey of Harvard announced that though Harvard "deplored" invoking the

Fifth Amendment as "entirely inconsistent with the candor to be expected of one devoted to the pursuit of truth," Harvard did not consider it an automatic reason for dismissal. Senator McCarthy quickly dubbed the Harvard faculty "Pusey's Fifth Amendment Communists."

At Rutgers University, however, in spite of a special faculty committee's recommendation to the contrary, the board of trustees ordered two professors dismissed unless they answered the questions of the Senate Internal Security Subcommittee as to whether they were or ever had been members of the Communist Party. Said the trustees, "The refusal of a faculty member, on the ground of possible self-incrimination, to answer [such] questions . . . impairs confidence in his fitness to teach. It is also incompatible with the standards required of him as a member of his profession."

At New York University, a professor who had refused to answer questions about his alleged membership in the Communist Party was suspended with pay, and a faculty committee was appointed to begin its own investigation of his fitness to teach. Called before the faculty committee, the professor declared that the evidence against him was irrelevant and denounced his accusers as professional witnesses. He also insisted that his colleagues had no business prying into his extracurricular activities. The committee disagreed. After 17 sessions and 984 pages of testimony, it made its report, and the professor was fired. Said Chancellor Henry T. Heald, "Refusal of a member of a faculty to answer questions put to him by his university in an effort to determine whether he is bound by commitments which violate his own academic freedom renders him unfit to continue in a position of educational trust."

More important, perhaps, than the individual case was the effect that charges of Communism had on bringing about conformity and discouraging independent thought. Harold Taylor, president of Sarah Lawrence College, responded by defining a patriotic American as: "One who tells his secrets without being asked, believes we should go to war with Russia, holds no political view without prior consultation with his employer, does not ask for increases in salary or wages, and is in favor of peace, universal military training, brotherhood, and baseball."

In 1955, a Ford Foundation unit was established to encourage political discussion groups on campuses. It was not until 1957—coincidentally the year of Joseph McCarthy's death—that any sign of "normal youthful reactions" appeared. By then President Eisenhower made his famous speech appealing to students to go into the libraries to study the *Communist Manifesto* and other Communist documents to acquaint themselves with the forces that were aligned against democracy.

The Fifties will be remembered as the decade of the panty raid. The rites of spring were celebrated by mass assaults on coed dorms for lingerie. The ingredients necessary were: a nice warm spring evening (preferably just before examinations), a nearby women's dormitory, and some cooperative girls who were willing to toss panties, bras, and slips out of their windows to the eager throng below. Earlier decades had witnessed such spectacles, but not so many, so widespread, or so cooperative.

At the University of Missouri in the spring of 1952, some 2,000 boys invaded not only the girls' dorm on their own campus, but proceeded to nearby Stephens College. Bags of the collected treasures were assembled the next day at the Missouri basketball court for return to the rightful owners.

Within one week there were similar panty raids at Michigan, Nebraska, Miami, Iowa, and a host of other places. Football players successfully defended the fortresses at the University of Georgia at Athens by blocking the entrances, but some girls who didn't want to be protected tossed lingerie out of their windows, others tossed water. Counterattacks took place at the University of Toledo, where girls raided a male dorm for shorts.

Once they got started, the panty raids were difficult to stop, and some got completely out of hand. At the University of Massachusetts the boys not only invaded the dormitories collecting souvenirs from dresser drawers, but they started to collect them from live bodies before the police force could end the affair. At Berkeley a rampage through sorority houses resulted in $10,000 damage. The student newspaper reported that girls were "knocked around, assaulted, carried outside in pajamas or nude." An editorial condemned the raid as a "night of debauchery." At the University of Ohio, the Athens police had to resort to tear gas to break up the riot. New York's Finest tried to defend the gates of Barnard College at Broadway and 116th Street with no help whatsoever from the girls, who were encouraging the boys not to give up by waving panties at their windows.

No one has counted how many students were arrested, jailed, dismissed, suspended, or put on probation as a result of such activities. Some girls were punished also, for giving the enemy too much encouragement. When Dr. Alfred Kinsey was asked for his insight on panty raids, he responded, "Campus riots are a long and psychological problem. It is somewhat out of my field."

Not all the student rampages involved panties. A practice air raid drill at Princeton turned into a mob scene on Nassau Street as 1,000 Princetonians stormed and broke up the show at the Garden Theater and a movie house. Before the evening was over they had managed to overturn several cars at the railroad station and every garbage can in sight. They did not, however, receive a warm reception at Westminister Choir College a mile away. Instead of panties, the girls threw pillows and shower curtains down at them. The evening ended abruptly at 12:30 A.M. when the dean finally caught up with the crowd and read the riot act.

At Harvard in 1952, a "Pogo for President" rally turned into a riot with the Cambridge police. When the students at the Yale campus took sides in an argument between two ice cream men about where they would set up their carts, fistfights broke out, and the full-scale riot required the services of the New Haven riot squad and fire department to put down.

The madness of the Fifties was not confined to riots and panty raids. There was the piano-wrecking craze, the object of which was to see who could most quickly smash a piano into pieces small enough to pass through a hole just under eight inches in diameter. Wayne State apparently held the record at 10 minutes 44.4 seconds. Telephone-booth jamming became a major fad. Seventeen squeezed in at U.C.L.A.; 32 students made it into the booth at Modesto Junior College in California to claim the record. Southeast Missouri State College insists that it holds the record at 35 students, but witnesses and photographs throw doubt on the validity of how many were actually inside the booth.

In the Fifties, styles and clothing fads were no longer launched at Harvard, Princeton, or Yale, as they had been. Now, they came from any part of the United States. But college dress was also more of a uniform than it had been, and you couldn't tell a Grinnell from a Harvard student by his dress. For the college man a gray flannel suit was a must. Sports jackets in a navy-blue flannel, in plaid, or check were popular. Blue blazers with gold metallic buttons became popular. In 1950 the tattersall vest was an Eastern fad moving West. Pink button-down shirts were being worn and hats were beginning to come back "in." Casual wear in the Eastern schools had the "studied sloppy" look.

To provide the air of insouciance that Ivy Leaguers are supposed to enjoy, the Harvard Coop started selling "Dusty Bucks," white shoes that had been specially treated to look ever so slightly worn and ever so slightly dirty.

At the Big Ten, corduroy pants and shirts were part of the standard wardrobe. On special occasions, students painted pictures or words on their pants. At Purdue some students wore them painted all year round. Fellows wore loud sport shirts, but the fad in the mid-Fifties at the Big Ten ran to colorful suède or capeskin jackets. In the Southwest, as evidence of the Indian influence, squaw boots and pastel bucks were the fashion instead of loafers.

The college girl of the Fifties wore sweaters and shirts, jeans, bermudas, loafers, and wool dresses. There was also a Madras fad. Skirts were getting shorter in the 1950s, and so were coiffures. The "Italian" haircut became the vogue. This style called for a short, carefully casual cut that gave the wearer a gamin-like, wind-blown look that was at the same time strikingly sophisticated. By 1959 the "sack" was the most discussed fashion, and short formals were in style everywhere.

A study sponsored by the National Committee on Fraternities in Education entitled *Fraternities Without Brotherhood* by Alfred McClung Lee reported that the number of national fraternity chapters more than doubled from World War II to 1956 and that further growth was expected, paralleling the increase of college enrollments. At the same time many of the nationals were under pressure from the locals to remove restrictive clauses from their constitutions. Some evaded the pressure by transferring the restrictions to their secret rituals.

Pressure for removing restrictive clauses had come immediately after the war. In 1946 the Middlebury (Vermont) chapter of Alpha Sigma Phi initiated four Jewish students in spite of the ritual that excluded membership on the basis of race and religion. Refusing to abide by the wishes of the national elders, Middlebury's Alpha Sigma Phi surrendered its charter and reconstituted itself at Alpha Sigma Psi. Similarly Amherst's Phi Kappa Psi's in 1948 pledged the Negro cross-country runner, Thomas W. Gibbs, and refused to de-pledge him at the insistence of the elders and reconstituted itself as a local Phi Alpha Phi. The chief consequences and benefits were that the new local saved $1,000 a year in dues to to the national.

In 1946 the Phi Mu Delta chapter at the University of New Hampshire pledged the son of a Massachusetts judge, and he moved into the fraternity house. Then the college dean advised fraternity members that because the man was Jewish they should clear his eligibility with the national organization. The national ordered the chapter to cancel his pledge and to move the man out of the house. Dr. Alfred McClung Lee quotes a chapter member's description of this grisly episode: "It was awful . . . The kid's parents came to help move him to the dormitory. I remember how terrible it was. His mother was crying. But what was worse was his father. That man didn't say a word to anyone."

"We have a war on our hands," Brother Lloyd C. Cochran, past president of the National Interfraternity Council, warned the troops of Alpha Sigma Phi in 1954. "We find student organizations which are reaching over the fence of their prerogative and telling us how to run our fraternities and how to establish our membership requirements. We find aloof and unfriendly college administrators, not appreciating the ideals and values that a fraternity should bring, who put stumbling blocks in our way." Actually it was the students rather than the administrators who were pressing for change. Most administrators were being scrupulously neutral and status quo. But the students under the pressure of student referenda were threatening to go local unless "the national gets rid of all this Caucasian-Christian crap."

The smaller private colleges such as Amherst, Williams, Middlebury, Dartmouth, and Allegheny shouldered a disproportionate share of the task of pioneering desegregation on American campuses. The big state universities had long been strongholds of the national fraternity system, and they were more difficult to crack. But even here, change was taking place. At the University of Minnesota, for instance, a poll of all fraternity men and sorority women in 1948 showed 58 percent favoring removal of racial and religious membership restrictions. By 1951, 83 percent of the fraternity men bound by such restrictions and 89 percent of those without them favored their removal.

In 1947 the National Interfraternity Council president, Brother David A. Embury, announced his determination to "fight to the last ounce of my strength to defend the right—the democratic right—of any man or group of men to form a fraternity . . . a fraternity of blacks for blacks, of whites for whites, of Jews for Jews, of Gentiles for Gentiles, of Catholics for Catholics, of Protestants for Protestants." After the Amherst case in 1948, a concerted drive to liberalize fraternities began on numerous campuses, chiefly at the instigation of the returning veterans, who had a pretty definite idea about what they'd been fighting for and against. Taken for granted before the war, fraternities suddenly came under severe scrutiny as to their usefulness as a part of the educational process.

The alignment of forces was a postwar generation of students that was overwhelmingly against the discrimination practiced by most of the national fraternities and sororities. Standing with the students were a few private and public college authorities who wanted to root out the weeds of institutionalized snobbism and prejudice that had flourished too long on the campuses. Against them were a small group of strategically placed elder brothers and elder sisters who held the mortgages on the fraternity houses, attended all the conventions, and often served as trustees of the college.

Many administrators were silent or unsupporting of the notion of desegregating the fraternities. In 1951, Alexander G. Ruthve, then president of the University of Michigan, said, "We do not believe . . . that the University could, without discrimination, withdraw recognition and thus jeopardize vested property interests merely because the organization was unwilling or unable to waive its legal right to define in its constitution the qualifications of its members." Even as late as 1953, Carl R. Woodward, president of the University of Rhode Island, asserted, "Under our American concept of freedom and self-determination selective membership is in keeping with the democratic institutions of our society, and the right of our fraternities to retain it should be protected." The college authorities who made efforts to change fraternity rules were a small minority. Of the 125 institutions surveyed by the National Committee on Fraternities in Education, 95 expressed no interest in the problem. Most of those that did express an interest were attempting to reform the national fraternities while retaining them on the campus. Their efforts ranged all the way from mild persuasion to ultimate giving a local chapter a "deadline for democracy."

During the middle Fifties, some nationals were successfully evading the issues of discrimination by subterfuge, that is, by expunging written discriminatory clauses from their secret rituals. Phi Delta Theta, for instance, voted at their convention to substitute "social accept-ability" for "non-Aryan." In 1954, a group of brothers met at the Edgewater Beach Hotel in Chicago to recommend that national fraternities actively take up cudgels against the anti-discrimination movement, even to the extent of boycotting campuses where it cropped up. The National Interfraternity Council did not go along with the Edgewater Beach conference's recommendations, but it did vote bouquets for several college administrations who had refused student demands for action against "the clauses."

Among the complaints of the elders was that the newer generation of fraternity men didn't have the "true" fraternity feeling. McLean C. Russell, executive secretary of Alpha Delta Phi, said, "Kids don't come to college nowadays with any preconceived ideas about fraternities—no particular affiliation through their parents, for instance, with the idea of a fraternity." If they do happen to join a fraternity, they aren't exactly seized in the faith—an experience that lawyer Russell Dock, an old Kappa Alpha, described as being "so prenatal that you don't know what it is."

Whatever it was, however, it wasn't any longer. The fraternity men of the Fifties had their hands full—with their elder brothers.

Television was the major form of entertainment of the early Fifties, and it was dominated by such shows as "I

Love Lucy." No wonder this generation was silent; it was trained not to speak until the commercials went on.

Water-skiing became a popular sport for the first time in 1958. Masses of students were beginning to converge on Fort Lauderdale during spring vacation (two years later *Where the Boys Are* was published, a novel depicting this rather hedonistic annual exodus), and Harvard Professor Kenneth Galbraith's *The Affluent Society* was published.

The popular music of the Fifties was uninspired. The top popular tunes in 1950 were "Good Night, Irene," "Music, Music, Music," "My Foolish Heart," and "Mona Lisa." The succeeding years produced "I Went to Your Wedding," "The Yellow Rose of Texas," and "Mr. Sandman." Then Elvis Presley hit the scene with "Hound Dog," "Love Me Tender," and in 1957 Pat Boone was approaching Presley in popularity with "Tammy," "Fascination," "Young Love" and "Round and Round." Rock and roll dominated even college music by 1956. By 1958 top popular songs were led by rock-and-roll "Purple People-Eater" and "Bird Dog," and the ballads were "A Certain Smile" and "Your Precious Love."

On the other hand, twenty-three-year-old pianist Van Cliburn won the Tchaikovsky International Piano and Violin Festival held in Moscow with his playing of Rachmaninoff's *Third Piano Concerto*. Folksongs were moving into the realm of popular music in 1959 with "Tom Dooley," "Stagger Lee," "The Battle of New Orleans," and "He's Got the Whole World in His Hands."

The memorable tunes came from Broadway musicals such as *South Pacific, Pajama Game, Kismet, West Side Story,* and *My Fair Lady*. College students were humming or dancing to: "Some Enchanted Evening," "Hey There," "Stranger in Paradise," "I Could Have Danced All Night," and "Tonight."

College tastes in listening to music were special, probably due to the technical perfection of recording devices—stereo came in in 1958. If students liked Beethoven, they wanted to hear recordings only of Toscanini. If they wanted hot jazz, it had to be either the original Dixieland Jazz Band or such ultra-moderns as Stan Kenton, the Dave Brubeck Quartet, or Norman Granz and his Jazz Philharmonic. "They go in for kicks," one record dealer explained. Translated from "collegese," this meant they went on a kind of musical binge for one thing only which might last for weeks on end.

If Beethoven quartets were the fad, only the performance of the world-famous Budapest Quartet would make them happy. If it was musical comedy, only the original cast recording would satisfy them. In the field of folk music, bagpipes and Folkways albums of native tunes of China, Japan, Ireland, the Caribbean Islands, and Armenia were favorites. Perhaps the most astonishing best seller in collegiate history turned up at the University-owned cooperative record shop in Princeton, New Jersey, where a Columbia album of "The Liturgy in English, According to the Uses of the Episcopal Church" became a leading item for months.

Stunned by TV, Hollywood throughout the decade presented the most beautiful and the handsomest in everything from *Rawhide* (Tyrone Power and Susan Hayward) to *Picnic* (Kim Novak and William Holden). Most of the films, designed for the adolescent "going out" crowd, seem creampuffs today, and one angry-looking James Dean could hardly counterbalance all the lightweights, led by Tab Hunter. Were the best American motion pictures all Westerns and gangster shows in this decade—*Shane, On the Waterfront, High Noon?* Were the only meaningful films those from abroad—such as *The Seventh Seal* (Bergman) and *La Strada* (Fellini)?

In looking at undergraduate attitudes, particularly with regard to literary heroes, Carlos Baker suggested that this was the Age of Consolidation. A most striking characteristic was that there were relatively few new gods. College students were too busy reading older writers and thinkers to pay much attention to the newest ones.

The quality paperback industry surfaced in the mid-1950s, and the scramble was on to publish sociology (Riesman's *The Lonely Crowd*), the Existentialists, history, science—all for the college market and soon for the general public as well. University presses began to roll out a different line of stock—not only the treatise but the important studies of past and present. The college bookshop came into its own.

Jack Kerouac, with his *On the Road* (1957) and his clique of young California poets, launched the Beatniks, an anti-Establishment movement, meager in numbers and influence in comparison with the Hippies of the Sixties. But the signs of a pop culture and message were already evident in arts that would make their full impact in the 1960s. Fellini, Samuel Beckett, Ingmar Bergman, Berthold Brecht, and other European dramatists and film-makers of the 1950s would become the enthroned gods of the 1960s, among campus intellectuals.

Albert Camus was now being read from coast to coast because he summed up in some way "the myth of the modern man" or embodied a sense of the "present-day predicament." Sartre and André Malraux were discovered also, ten years after they were published in France. Existentialism penetrated even more broadly in the Sixties.

Of the writers writing about youth, the students of the Fifties particularly ready J. D. Salinger and Thomas Wolfe.

Many read D. H. Lawrence, James Joyce, and Dylan Thomas. William Faulkner's college following became something of a cult. And for reasons other than literary, Ayn Rand had a tremendous following in the late Fifties. Professor George R. Stewart summed up this generation as follows: ". . . there is far too little sense of excitement, of eager and rebellious youth. Someone should let loose a literary bomb that would blow the whole situation to pieces and put us into a state of flux again. If something of the sort doesn't happen soon, the undergraduate generation following this one may well never escape from childhood involvement with the blandishments of TV and the other mass media."

CHAPTER VI

THE KENNEDY IDEAL, 1960–1963

CLARK KERR, president of the University of California at Berkeley, prophesied in 1959 about the student generation of the Sixties: "I can just see . . . that they are not going to press many grievances . . . they are going to do their jobs, they are going to be easy to handle. There aren't going to be riots. There aren't going to be revolutions. There aren't going to be many strikes."

As everyone now knows, Kerr was wrong, but no one knew to what extent. And no educator in his wildest moments would have guessed what the decade of the Sixties would bring to Berkeley in particular and American higher education in general.

The Sixties brought to the American colleges commitment, involvement, relevance, and pot. It brought participatory democracy, student evaluation of professors, student involvement in the decision-making process, the end of academic credit for R.O.T.C. The Sixties brought mass take-overs of classroom buildings, administrative offices, and computer centers, fires in libraries, clashes with police, confrontation with the National Guard. It produced a backlash of state legislators, members of Congress, the courts, the general public, parents, alumni, and academic administrators. The richness of the Sixties brought the idealism, style, graciousness, and dedication of J.F.K. It also brought cynicism and disgust with war, the draft, the System, and a greater awareness of the anomie of human existence in modern society. The Sixties brought a larger and more talented student body than ever before. It also brought students who questioned the values on which the academic community was built, its structure and basic rationale for continuing.

While the Sixties brought the reality of reaching the moon and the ability to harness man's knowledge in computers, it also created in the young people a questioning of human values and a questioning of what is "self." As the affluent society sent its children to college, there developed, less and less, the pragmatic desire to get through with college in order to make a good living, and increasingly the questioning of the fundamental moral values and basic fiber of our society. For all the accomplishments of satellite launchings and the successes of American science, there was on the other side the assassinations of President John F. Kennedy, Martin Luther King, Jr., and still another young Kennedy—Robert.

If the decade started as the age of innocence, with a belief in the immediate betterment of man, the second half of the Sixties saw the end of that. It was the end of the good and bad. As the Sixties concluded, college students sensed with distress the complexity of the life around them. The students of the Sixties searched and they searched hard for meaning in their lives—existentially they sought for answers, in a piece of action, being part of the scene, being just plain "with it."

They drove college administrators, faculties, state legislators, Congress, and even the President of the United States to the point of distraction with the chaos, bloodshed, and disruption on the campuses. They refused to conform, insisted upon "doing their own thing," and seemed in general totally uncontrollable. College was always fun to the older generation—why should this generation take it so earnestly, why should it take it so belligerently, why should it question the values accepted so easily by the previous generations?

The mood of the early Sixties for American College life was established with the inauguration of John F. Kennedy. Here was a symbol not only of youthfulness but also of idealism and commitment. And if any single person was needed to follow the silent age of the Fifties, John F. Kennedy was the man. When Kennedy introduced the Peace Corps, he was challenging the student generation. When Kennedy spoke of discrimination and racial prejudice, he was speaking to the college generation who wanted to do something about it. When Kennedy spoke the words of his inaugural speech, "Ask not what your country can do for you, ask what you can do for your country," he spoke to the student generation—and they followed him. So it was—whether or not one should generalize it in terms of cause and effect—that the student movement coincides historically, at least in the time frame, with John F. Kennedy.

It began with a happening—the sit-in movement that swept the country. A bull session about the racial situation at a dormitory room of predominantly Negro North Carolina Agricultural and Technical College in Greensboro resulted in a simple plan. On February 1, 1960, four black freshmen entered a Woolworth store and each purchased a tube of toothpaste, an act perfectly acceptable by local mores. But then, they sat at the lunch counter and requested coffee. "I'm sorry, we don't serve colored here," was the response. The young Negroes remained at the counter until closing time. The sit-in movement had started. Within a few weeks sit-in demonstrations were taking place in many parts of North Carolina—Raleigh, Winston-Salem, Salisbury, Concord, Durham, and Charlotte. In Virginia they took place in Richmond, Portsmouth, and Hampton. Nonviolence workshops and seminars were started to prepare students for lunch counter confrontation. According to Howard Zinn in *The New Abolitionists,* more than 50,000 people participated in some kind of civil rights protest in the twelve months after Greensboro and over 3,600 demonstrators spent time in jail.

What started in the South was quickly picked up with enthusiasm on Northern campuses. Thousands of Northern white and Negro students joined in sympathy picket lines at Woolworth stores in urban areas. Others who were more venturesome—and there were thousands—drove, took buses, or hitchhiked to the South to participate in sit-ins, marches, boycotts, and voter registration drives. Nonviolent civil disobedience as a form of protest against racial discrimination caught the imagination of college students from coast to coast and they responded energetically. The lethargy of the silent Fifties was quickly shaken off, and this new movement grew spontaneously and contagiously.

"We Shall Overcome" became the anthem of the civil rights movement, and later President Johnson concluded a nationwide broadcast with those words.

College demonstrators and freedom marchers sang "The Berlin Wall" (to the tune of "Joshua Fit the Battle of Jericho"), "Fighting for My Rights," "Free at Last," (Martin Luther King's favorite spiritual), "Oh, Freedom" (a spiritual dating from the Civil War), "We Shall Not Be Moved" (an old union song), and "Which Side Are You

On" (an old union song, with freedom verses added, some written by James Farmer of CORE, the Congress of Racial Equality).

In August 1964 the country was electrified when three civil rights workers were murdered in Mississippi, two of them Northern white college boys. In October, Martin Luther King was awarded the Nobel Peace Prize, and in March 1965 he led the Selma, Alabama, demonstration. Many thousands of high school and college students joined the Washington March soon after, a vast dignified assemblage of blacks and whites led by King to influence Congress to pass civil rights legislation.

As Jack Newfield says in *A Prophetic Minority*, ". . . the sit-ins were a heroic innovation, fulfilling the students' taste for drama and novelty. Behind the sit-in technique was the pacifist ethics of placing one's body in moral nonviolent confrontation with an existing evil. The Freedom rides, the pilgrimages to Mississippi, the community-organizing projects, are all an extension of this principle of direct moral confrontation."

This was the students' movement. They moved it as only they could, with moral commitment and fervor, with youthful idealism and lack of concern for themselves or their future. They moved as only they could, spurred by the aura surrounding a youthful President under whose leadership idealistic things might be possible. And thus, almost overnight, student unions with all their facilities—bowling alleys, Ping Pong tables, billiard tables, dance floors, ballrooms, conference rooms—became somehow irrelevant. Extracurricular activities quickly responded to the changing times as the student's interests turned outside to the community. The Citizenship Program at Columbia began to send over a thousand student volunteers each week into Harlem and other New York City slums to tutor students or work with the aged, drug addicts, and the mentally handicapped. They volunteered at hospitals, prisons, political offices, city and state agencies. Throughout the country at hundreds of colleges and universities, volunteer social action programs became more popular than traditional club activities. Extracurricular activities were no longer dominated by a series of sensations without commitment. No longer was it meaningful to have student governments to practice democracy, when the real-life challenges were right before them. On a number of campuses, student governments were abolished. A chance to make a difference, an obligation to serve society even at the same time that one was in college, these were the motivating forces for the student of the early Sixties. A sense of involvement in, and commitment to, the world outside permeated the campuses.

The causes that students championed often seemed more moral than political. Civil rights was a crusade with its sit-ins and Freedom Rides. The tactic of passive resistance lent a Gandhiesque color to the other causes—the abolishment of capital punishment, HUAC (House Un-American Activities Committee), banning the bomb. The mood was contagious and effective in its dignity. When college students went to Washington to picket for peace at the White House, President Kennedy sent out a five-gallon urn of coffee. U.C.L.A. students voted to send $5,000 to buy appeal bonds for five jailed Freedom Riders in Mississippi, as college students became involved with voter registration projects in the South, particularly under the leadership of Student Nonviolent Coordinating Committee (SNCC).

But then John F. Kennedy was assassinated. And symbolically, if not historically, that ended the dream and the belief in the words "We Shall Overcome." The anguish of Kennedy's death brought with it the end of an age of innocence, the belief that there is a good and a bad and that the good conquers in the end, the belief that the good conquers if one works hard enough.

Larry L. King wrote of the Kennedy influence in *Harper's Magazine* in April 1968:

> We needed something. Kennedy gave it to us. Call it a sense of Style. Suddenly America might be believed again. It might grow young. Its liver spots might disappear. It might reach the moon and other higher destinies: young men and women of many races and classes joined hands in the bloodier thickets of the South and sang their hope. We Shall Overcome. Our youth invaded distant lands not with flamethrowers and guns but as missionaries of the Peace Corps. Appalachia would come to life; Martin Luther King would have his dream; America was on the move again. How incredibly naive it all seems today, and how quickly it passed.

What was interesting about the early Sixties was that the trend toward greater activism was also taking place on the political Right. Editor Peter Stuart of the Michigan *Daily* observed in 1961: "The signs point to a revival of interest in individualism and decentralization of power— principles espoused by John Locke and Thomas Jefferson and rekindled by Senator Barry Goldwater." Interestingly, the reason given by many students for turning to the conservative movement was the rebellion against conformity.

As evidence of the turn to the political Right, *Time* pointed to the fact that Goldwater's *Conscience of a Conservative* was a best seller at 200 colleges. Young Americans for Freedom, which was founded in 1960, had a reported membership of 21,000 on 115 campuses by 1961. William F. Buckley, Jr., author of *God and Man at Yale* and editor of the conservative magazine *National Review,* became a popular speaker on college campuses. This new conservative trend was to culminate in the nomination of

When Men Were Men and Girls Came into Their Own...

1. 1900, Kentucky State College

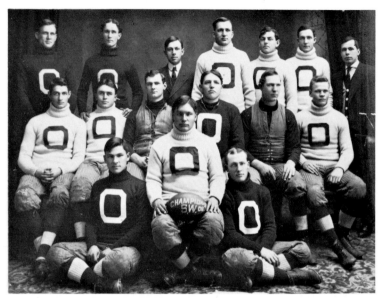

2. 1908, Championship Football Team, Indian captain, University of Oklahoma

3. 1910, Women's Basketball Team, University of Michigan

4. 1914, Basketball Team, Skidmore College

5. 1915, Wellesley Crew

Spring Rites

6. Hoop Roll, Wellesley, 1900

7. May Queen, Sweet Briar, 1929

8. Maypole, Sweet Briar, 1915

9. "Engagement Ring," Sweet Briar, 1958

10. Daisy Chain, Vassar, 1915

11. Dancing on the Green, Skidmore, 1920

12. "The Awakening of Princess Daffodil," Sweet Briar, 1912

Dormitories

13. 1900, Kentucky State College

14. 1913, Mount Holyoke College

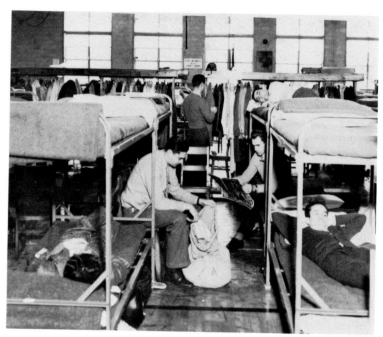

15. 1946, G.I. Bunks, Jenison Gym, Michigan State University

16. Quonsets, married student housing, 1947, Michigan State University

The Top and the Bottom, Bennett College

17. 1904 Pompadour   18. 1917 "Goddess" style

19. 1910 "Rats" and fluff

20. 1918 Irene Castle cut

21. 1927 Shingle bob

22. 1935 Short curls

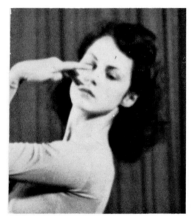

23. 1942 Long and curled

24. 1952 Short, curled under

25. 1968 Long, often stringy

26. 1910 Dirty tennis shoes (later called "sneakers")

27. 1910 Slippers

28. 1910 High button shoes
Blackstone

29. 1915 Black stockings, ribbon-tied oxfords

30. 1915 White-laced walking shoes

31. 1920 Galoshes

32. 1927 Groundgrippers

33. Early 1930s Ghillies

34. 1936 Saddle shoes

35. 1946 Bobby sox and loafers, saddle shoes

36. 1955 Ballet slippers

37. 1968 Leather boots

The Style

38. 1903 Gibson girls, Bennett College

39. 1912 Stiff collar, four-button jacket, Boston University

40. 1915 College uniform required, Loretta Heights, Denver

41. 1918 Irene Castle look,
Bennett College

42. 1922 Flapper, collar and sweater, Bennett College

43. 1926 Best dressed man, Columbia

44. 1928 Raccoon coat, Wellesley

United Press International

45. 1938 Bobby soxers, Bennett College

46. 1945 "Shirttail out," Wellesley

47. 1969 Maxicoat, miniskirt, Boston University

48. 1969 Afro and bush jacket, Boston University

49. 1969 Long hair, beard, bull-horn, Boston University

Never on Foot

50. 1926 Ford, Georgia Tech

51. Ford, circa 1921, Straight College, New Orleans (later Dillard University)

52. 1937 Antique bike craze, Oberlin

53. 1965 Parking prank, Wooster Polytechnic Institute
United Press International

54. 1969 Bikes outside class, Oberlin

55. 1969 Motorcycles, University of Texas

Traditions: Universal and Local

56. Circa 1900, textbook burning, on completion of semester, Purdue

57. The "cord" tradition since 1904, Purdue

58. 1907 Prom (without men), Bennett College

59. 1960's Student rodeo, Montana State at Bozeman

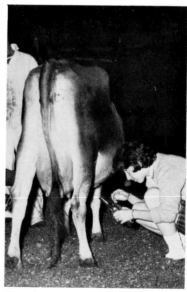

60. Annual fair, Coke-bottle milking, University of Kentucky

61. 1905 to present day, Whitewashing the "U," University of Utah

62 and 63. Tappan Square Rock painting at Oberlin, every two weeks, by anyone. Above, Santa Claus and Eugene McCarthy Campaign 1968

64 and 65. Soph-Frosh Rush, Columbia. Left, Greased Pole.
Right, Giant Push Ball, 1947

66. Soph-Freshman tug of war, Cal. Tech. 52nd annual event,
1967

Fads and Follies

67. Telephone booth craze, 35 Southeast State collegians, April 1959 *Wide World Photos*

68. Goldfish swallowing, 24th going down, Harvard, March 1939 *Wide World Photos*

69. Molasses and feathers, student body president, Willamette University, Oregon, October 1966 *Wide World Photos*

70. Dormitory bed piling, 72 Fresno State collegians, May 1961 *Wide World Photos*

71. Pie-eating contest, Montana State University at Bozeman, 1968

72. Pre-game bonfire, Stanford University, 1945

73. Panty raid, University of Nebraska, May 1952

Wide World Photos

74. Sport car crush, 31 Lambda Chi Alphas, Lancaster, Pa., 1959

Wide World Photos

Coed Music

75. 1900 Mount Holyoke Mandolin Club

76. 1930 Girls' Band, University of Kentucky

77. 1960 Sorority sing, University of Kentucky

Greek Traditions

78. 1911 Greek charioteers, Columbia

79. 1913 Greek eternal fire, Barnard

80. 1914 Greek charioteers, Barnard

81. Early 50s Greek charioteers, Barnard

82. 1960s Annual Greek Week Olympics, chariot race, University of Utah

Wartime Campus

83. Barnard nurse training, World War I

84. Wellesley Farmerettes, 1918

85. Wellesley Land Army Training Camp, World War I

86. Cadet Officers, Agricultural and Mechanical College of Kentucky (later the University), 1897

87. Student Army Training Corps combat practice, University of Denver, 1918

88. Army Specialized Training Program graduation, World War II, University of Denver

89. Skidmore Victory Gardens, 1943

90. Earliest college WAC induction, Sweet Briar College, April 1944

91. Korean WAVE induction, Skidmore, 1951

Social Action, Early 1960s

92. JFK White House address to first Peace Corps volunteers, August, 1961

93. Civil rights and anti-civil rights student pickets, Greensboro, North Carolina, 1960

Wide World Photos

94. James Meredith attending first class on Supreme Court order, University of Mississippi, October 1962

Wide World Photos

95. Temple University student, Philippine rice paddy, Peace Corps, 1969

"Ins" of the Late 60s

96. Teach-in, Queens College, New York, May 1965. All-night session with students and teachers discussing Vietnam

Wide World Photos

97. Nude-in, Grinnell College, protesting speech by *Playboy* speaker

98. Tree-in, blocking removal of trees, University of Texas, October 1969

United Press International

Student Power

99. Mario Savio addressing rally at Berkeley, December 1964
United Press International

100. Student volunteers for Eugene McCarthy, New Hampshire primary, March 1968

Wide World Photos

101. President S. I. Hayakawa personally disconnecting student sound truck, San Francisco State College, December 1968

Wide World Photos

102. Afro-American Society demonstrators, Cornell University, April 1969

United Press International

Anti-War

103. October 18, 1967. Students protest Dow Chemical Company job interviews at University of Wisconsin because they manufacture napalm for Vietnam War

Wide World Photos

104. October 26, 1967. Students surround car of U.S. Naval recruit

berlin

105. February 13, 1968. Berkeley student, opposed to Anti-ROTC demonstration

Associated Press

106. April 29, 1969. Anti-ROTC demonstration, Tulane University

United Press International

107. October 15, 1969. Guerrilla Theater presentation, Moratorium Day, University of Pennsylvania

Photo by Frank Ross, Chronicle of Higher Education

108. October 1, 1968. Dissenting soldier given sanctuary, Marsh Chapel, Boston University

109. November 1969. Washington Peace March

Barry Goldwater at the Republican convention of 1964.

In the early Sixties the movement from the Left was still a movement *for* something: *for* desegregation, *for* equality for the blacks, *for* individualism. It still was not, at least not perceptively, a movement *against* impersonalization, a battle *against* the alienation in mass society, a revolt *against* the IBM card, or a rebellion *against* war. This change in tone was to come soon enough, sooner than one thought.

The Sixties were culturally a rich but incoherent decade. John and Jacqueline Kennedy represented elegance, graciousness, style, and culture in their White House parties, but the early Sixties also brought pop art, the trivia rage, and a Bat Man revival. The period of Lyndon B. Johnson summoned images of America the Beautiful with Ladybird Johnson dedicating blades of grass all over the country, keeping the highways clean, removing billboards—making America beautiful as the atmosphere clouded.

In many ways the late Fifties were the groundswell of the following decade. Folksingers had emerged from the oppressed atmosphere of the McCarthy period. Guitars were to be heard everywhere in the early 1960s at thousands of high school and college gatherings, as well as on radio and TV. The Grand Old Opry country music filled the air. A square-dance convention was held in Denver in 1959, and some estimated that a million young square-dancers were thronging the halls, church basements, and nightclubs. Hootenanny, also a phenomenon of the college scene in the late 1940s, appeared on ABC-TV. The folk tune "If I Had a Hammer" was a top hit for at least two years.

The Newport Folk Festival was only one of the many

that became an annual affair (Jean Ritchie's in Tennessee had been going for years).

The Madison, which began in the Negro section of Baltimore, became a dance craze in 1960, with a leader calling out the figures.

Along with folk music, jazz more than held its own. In 1959 there were eight major festivals. The first National Jazz Camp was held at the University of Indiana and jazz courses were given at the Universities of Michigan, Florida, Kansas, Texas, Colorado, and California. In 1960, colleges were the most important locations of small combos, and eleven major jazz festivals were held. This fell to seven the next year.

Beginning in 1961, it seemed that the Twist dominated popular dancing, and several hit songs were dedicated to it. Soon at college dances the Twist branched off into the Slop, the Mashed Potato, the Dirty Bird, and the Hully Gully, which was performed in square-dance formation, soon followed by the Dog, Monkey, and Slurp. From Trinidad came the Limbo (1963)—not so easy for the unathletic, as the dancer bent backward edging under a lowering pole. By 1964, the discothèque came in, with girls perpetually dancing (in one spot) the Watusi and dozens of variations. Op art was preparing the way for the psychedelic craze.

Film festivals spread from coast to coast. Brecht, Ionesco, Ingmar Bergman, Fellini, and Antonioni seemed to take all honors away from the American film. *La Dolce Vita* (Fellini) was the notable film of 1960. In 1959, 255 foreign films were released here, 233 in 1960, and 331 in 1961.

But the mood was changing. By 1963, rock and roll, which had been rumbling along since the mid-1950s, broke loose. The Beatles struck America, and their Liverpool sound would soon be evident across the land (see Chapter IX). Folk music merged into folk rock, and Bob Dylan (singing "Blowin' in the Wind"), Judy Collins, and others no longer called themselves folksingers. Gospel tunes were popular (soul music appeared later), and, in complete contrast, the new sport of surfriding inspired a rash of surf songs.

The age of restraint was going from publishing. By 1963 a New York court permitted the publication of *Fanny Hill,* and college administrators (the author among them) were confronted with four-letter words in campus publications. This was nothing compared to what was coming.

Princeton's humor magazine, *The Tiger,* died. Long a tradition at Princeton, and a magazine that F. Scott Fitzgerald wrote many a piece for, it was alas, now anachronistic.

Nothing really took the place of the college humor magazines, unless one wants to consider *Playboy.* The college sense of humor was changing. Deliberate absurdities raged through the college campuses in the early Sixties. There were the elephant jokes: What do you get when you cross an elephant with a jar of peanut butter? A peanut that never forgets or an elephant that sticks to the roof of your mouth. What goes thump, thump, thump, squish? An elephant with a wet sneaker.

Or the grape jokes: What's purple and hums? An electric grape. Why does it hum? It doesn't know the words. What is purple and has four beatles? Grape Britain.

Inspired by author Edward Stratemeyer's series, there were also the Tom Swifties: "I've been looking forward to this ride," said Lady Godiva shiftlessly.

A Pop game called Trivia, invented by Columbia students Dan Carlinsky and Ed Goodgold, was played by hundreds of thousands of college students. This national fad was a campy game of inconsequential questions and answers about radio, TV, movies, comic books, and popular songs. It included questions such as: "What were the names of Superman's parents on Krypton?" "What are the words to the Bosco jingle?" "Who were the inhabitants of Allen's Alley?" Trivia, according to Goodgold and Carlinsky, was composed of questions that produce "emotional responses to the non-monumental yet nostalgic events of those thrilling days of yesteryear. . . . It's enjoyed by those who have misspent their youth and don't want to let it go. It's the least common cultural denominator."

Other fads were skateboards, Bangasas (Japanese umbrellas), and love beads. Not to mention computerized match-making.

The Beatles have been blamed for the long-hair fad. It lasted straight through the Sixties, rendering crew cuts hard to find on the campus. College boys wore bangs down to the eyebrows, locks down to the shoulders. Some wore beards and mustaches. Others—less venturous—at least wore sideburns.

CHAPTER VII

THE STUDENT REVOLT, 1964–1969

A MINOR official made what would appear to be a minor decision. Specifically, the Dean of Students at Berkeley announced the decision that the solicitation of funds for off-campus political action groups would no longer be allowed on a 26-foot strip of land between Bancroft and Telegraph. From this minor decision arose one of the most important events in the history of American higher education. The Berkeley Student Revolt in 1964, being the first massive student revolution in America, shook the academic community to its foundations. The events that took place from September 14, 1964, to January 4, 1965, tore one campus apart in three months of crisis. Some educators around the country feared the repercussions of Berkeley on other campuses. But few would have guessed that by the end of the decade, student revolt would take place at hundreds of campuses.

This was the first major student confrontation using civil disobedience as a strategy—a strategy borrowed from sit-ins in the South. The spirit and strategy was described in a letter written by "a former student" and distributed with the *Slate Supplement Report* before the specific cause of "free speech" became an issue. The letter read:

The University does not deserve a response of loyalty and allegiance from you. There is only one proper response to

Berkeley from undergraduates: that you ORGANIZE AND
SPLIT THIS CAMPUS WIDE OPEN! . . .

Go to the top. Make your demands to the Regents. If they
refuse to give you an audience: start a program of agitation,
petitioning, rallies, etc., in which the final resort will be CIVIL
DISOBEDIENCE. In the long run, there is the possibility that
you will find it necessary to perform civil disobedience at a
couple of major University public ceremonies. . . .

The student protest movement was called the Free Speech
Movement (F.S.M.). Before the Berkeley revolt was over,
F.S.M. had not only drawn into the controversy the deans
and the president of the university, but also the governor,
the state legislature, and the entire state. Hundreds of
police were massed on the campus on at least two occasions,
and violence seemed inevitable. There were three sit-ins,
one culminating in the occupation of the central administration building by several hundred students who were
finally forcibly removed by an equal number of police. A
sympathy strike was organized by teaching assistants, and
classroom routines were interrupted. Although free speech
was a convenient and persuasive rallying cry, the Berkeley
revolt was concerned with deeper unrest on the campus.
Small specific issues broadened into questioning of the
whole structure and value system of the American university. The F.S.M. stood for the right of students to question: the purpose and nature of higher education; the rights,
freedoms, and responsibilities of students; the relevance
of the curriculum; the neglect of undergraduate education
and the alienation of students from faculty.

No small part of the impact that Berkeley had on the
nation was the fact that the questions raised were valid and
universal. Students were demanding more freedom both
inside and outside. This ranged from the abolition of
parietal rules, the concept of the university acting *in loco*

parentis, to a relaxing of curriculum requirements and the questioning of the grading system. Refusing to be treated like products on an assembly line, students conceived of learning as a process that would entail action and participation. This was an action-oriented generation that sought to make learning more meaningful. They objected to the lecture method, not only because classes had become too large, but also because of the role of the professor as an authority figure.

The students wanted to be part of the teaching-learning process and not just be the passive receptacles of "gems of knowledge." Students also distrusted a System that imposed on its end products—the graduates—certain fixed qualities and constrained them to live up to a narrowly conceived set of specifications. The Sixties produced students who challenged the "Establishment" and its "values," and made them household questions of all society. It was not willing to accept the values of the Organization Man in business or in education. The students sought to affirm their own individuality.

The response to the Berkeley riots by the academic community around the country was by and large positive and constructive. A Select Committee on Education at Berkeley was established in March 1965, chaired by Professor Charles Muscatine. In less than a year a final report was published containing 42 recommendations, among them suggestions for making the curriculum more relevant and personal. Berkeley, of course, was not alone in re-evaluating higher education. Throughout the country, faculties were goaded into action.

Berkeley had the largest undergraduate student body of any single institution in the country, and quite a few others had gone well over the 50,000 mark.

The first of the post-World War II baby boom were entering college in 1965, and the scramble to build and expand had hit the big state universities and all others who did not hold down their registrations. Not only were there more young people than ever before, but more were entering college. Only a third of the high school graduates went on to higher education before World War II; by the mid-1960s well over half were entering college. A new, typically American phenomenon appeared—the two-year community colleges, some of them built by hard-pressed counties even without state funds, some as branches of state multi-universities. By 1966, one and a half million were enrolled, or six times more than were registered in two-year colleges in 1950. These new campuses primarily served local students who commuted by car and bus, as they had in high school. As many as a third of all students are entering community colleges in 1970, with a thousand such campuses in operation.

Large universities, particularly public universities, were by the mid-Sixties being criticized for the neglect of teaching. To respond to the criticism that professors must "publish or perish," student evaluation of teaching performance became common. In October 1965 the Kahn Committee at Cornell University even suggested that the student "be given technical and financial aid in formulating questionnaires, analyzing results, and preparing and publishing a campus-wide evaluation of courses." Laura Kent in *The Education Record* reported:

At campuses around the country, course and teacher evaluation booklets are proliferating, sometimes with the approval of the administration and the faculty, but often without it. In the Washington area alone, student groups at Georgetown University, American University, George Washington University, the University of Maryland, Catholic University, and Howard University have published or are in the stages of planning to publish course evaluations. At C. C. N. Y., the University of Washington, the University of Michigan, and the University of Wisconsin, published guides have appeared during the past year.

This spate of "report cards" from students to teachers has been attended by a considerable amount of fanfare in the newspapers: "A NEW STUDENT REVOLT"; "FALLOUT FROM BERKELEY"; "THE BOOKWORM TURNS"; "SHAPE UP, PROF!"

Other topics discussed on campuses were: how to create a sense of college community; finding alternatives to lecturing; providing for student involvement in educational planning; reevaluation of the grading system; liberalizing the curriculum; developing courses with more "relevance" to students; giving students greater freedom to do independent study or field work.

"Innovation," "relevance," and "reform" were the key words on campuses and professional academic meetings. Yet much of it was merely talk, until students again led the way. "Free universities" where students taught non-credit courses on "relevant" subjects grew up all over the country.

To hundreds of thousands of college students, the old model of college education, of Mark Hopkins and his log, had no reality at all. Classes of 1,000 or more students were the rule rather than the exception; for many courses one often didn't have a class with a professor until the junior or senior year. All that was needed to surface this discontent was some kind of spark. Berkeley was it.

While the popularity of the teach-ins may have been enhanced by the novelty of curfew waivers for women, the enthusiasm, seriousness, and sense of academic community created by them on hundreds of college campuses during the mid-Sixties should not be underestimated.

It was a protest movement against the war in Vietnam. Professors—often professors of math, psychology, biology, and others who were not necessarily experts in foreign affairs—were willing to stay up all night in a crowded school auditorium to speak out on an issue that concerned students. What made it exciting was that professors took time off from their writing and research to show their humanistic concerns about an unjust war, about perceived immorality. To be sure, most of the teach-ins were one-sided—they were against the war in Vietnam. There were differences of opinion about whether teach-ins should be one-sided or whether they should be open-minded in the best academic tradition. But it was fundamentally a protest movement as originally conceived at the University of Michigan, and by and large, it remained that way.

Taking place in the evening and lasting all night at many campuses, the teach-ins sometimes had a carnival-like atmosphere. Teach-ins were picketed by pro-war students who waved banners and shouted obscenities at the speakers. Often, teach-ins were interrupted by fistfights and other disruptions by antagonistic groups. But also there was a sense of excitement and relevance, something that many students were experiencing for the first time in their academic careers. And they took place not only at Berkeley, Michigan, and Wisconsin, where one would expect such protests, but also at normally more subdued colleges like Marist College in Poughkeepsie, New York, Goucher College in Maryland, Kent State University in Ohio, and hundreds of others. On many campuses these events created a greater sense of academic community for students than college convocations, classes, or commencement.

Ignoring the phenomenon at first, the Federal government finally had to concede that the teach-in movement had picked up such a furious momentum that "truth squads" from the State Department and officials in Washington visited the campuses to respond to the charges laid to the U.S. Government. The very fact that the U.S. Government felt the need to respond to the teach-in revealed, in itself, the extent and successful impact of the teach-in as a protest movement.

It is doubtful that the movement had any effect on American foreign policy. Those who brought the protest movement to the next stage were convinced that it had not changed the nation's policies, and that other forms of protest were necessary.

By the time the teach-ins were in full swing, President Lyndon Baines Johnson was in trouble with the campus liberals—both student and faculty. They had been for him in the Presidential race against Barry Goldwater. They felt that he was the peace candidate. But now they felt betrayed. Bombings of North Vietnam started. Draft calls had grown larger. The defense budget was increasing at the same time that ghetto riots were taking place. The war in Vietnam was escalating and L.B.J.'s veracity was questioned as the credibility gap became an issue.

Perhaps it was just style. The Texan, well-known as a manipulator and wheeler-dealer in the U.S. Senate, was not what idealistic youngsters would have asked for. Lyndon Johnson showing the scar on his abdomen on national television after an operation was the antithesis of what one would call "style." The former English teacher was simply not communicating.

They had given him a chance, actually. In the remaining year of Kennedy's term of office, the campuses became quieter. Enthusiasm for the Peace Corps or the domestic version of the Peace Corps—VISTA—did not suffer from Kennedy's death. Five years after its birth, there were 10,380 Peace Corpsmen in 46 countries as compared to 526 volunteers in 13 countries in the initial year. Johnson's plea to "let us continue" was believed, despite the lack of identification with an older President.

If Johnson had had his way, he would have been a "domestic President." His theme had been the development of the "Great Society." More particularly his desire was to be remembered as the "Education President." Perhaps the college students would not have turned against him if it hadn't been for Vietnam. But the movement was increasingly focused upon demonstrations against the war in Vietnam, draft resistance, and sit-ins on Dow Chemical, military, and C.I.A. recruiters.

Youth, academicians, and intellectuals were dropping out of politics by the winter of 1968. Johnson was suffering an "inspiration gap." As the National Committee for an Effective Congress declared early in 1968, "America has experienced two great internal crises in her history: The Civil War and the economic depression of the 1930's. The country may now be on the brink of a third trauma, a depression of the national spirit."

The effect of the changing Johnson image on campus was profound. If Johnson had once been viewed as vital, clever, and shrewd, he was later seen as violent, devious, and cynical. The matter of style was not merely Harvard vs. Southwest Texas State Teachers at San Marcos. As Larry L. King wrote in *Harper's Magazine* (April 1968):

Can the apologists not understand that in a world searching for and needing greater truths, Style is directly related to credibility at home and abroad, to inspiring a nation or reassuring a world?

Do they not see that in a time when our cities burn, when our children "turn on, tune in, and drop out," when our young men die unexplained, when we have lost faith in the old virtues and do not yet fully trust the new, that only someone with a sense of Style can reach us?

A turning point occurred in 1965. In early August President Johnson announced the increase of troops in Vietnam and the doubling of the monthly draft quota. By fall, the protest against the war in Vietnam had mounted, with protest parades and chants such as, "Hey, hey, L.B.J.! How many kids did you kill today?" Campus protesters burned draft cards, ran fund drives for the Vietcong, and organized teach-ins. Berkely students even attempted to prevent troop trains from entering the Oakland Army Terminal. Max Lerner observed that "the idea of being patriotic seems to most of them square and laughable."

As the demonstrations stepped up, a counter-reaction also took place. A petition signed by 1,300 Harvard students stated that they "wish to disassociate (themselves) from the vocal minority which, distrusting American intentions, seeks to obstruct and misrepresent American policy." Other petitions, each with thousands of signatures supporting U.S. policy, came from the campuses of University of Texas, Southern Illinois, St. Louis, Yale, Stanford, Michigan State, Minnesota, and Princeton. "Bleed-ins" took place at Ohio State, Stanford, and many other campuses where blood drives for U.S. soldiers were organized. In Georgia, the organization Affirmation: Vietnam (A.V.N.) was formed, spread to 50 campuses in Georgia, and at its peak attracted 10,000 to a rally at Atlanta Stadium.

However, as the monthly draft calls rose to 30,000 and over, young men in college could no longer ignore the war in Vietnam. For the first time since the Korean War, a draftee might find himself on a battlefield. The escalation of the war caused draft boards to reclassify college students to 1A status as they sought to fill their quotas. So the class of 1966 found itself actually on the way to the fighting lines.

The air rang with anti-war songs old and new: "I Ain't Gonna Study War No More" (one of the most powerful of all spirituals), "Where Have All the Flowers Gone" (Pete Seeger's haunting words and melody), "The Cruel War Is Raging" (by Peter, Paul and Mary), and "Draft Dodger Rag" (Phil Ochs).

By the spring of 1967, the "Hell No, We Won't Go" movement was spreading swiftly from coast to coast. Martin Luther King, Jr., was mobilizing 10,000 volunteers for his "Vietnam Summer" aimed at educating against the war. Members of SNCC (Student Nonviolent Coordinating Committee) were refusing induction. The Draft Resistance Movement, organized to advise students how to resist the draft, was starting to pick up steam. Draft counsellors aided potential draftees in identifying legitimate deferments: homosexual tendencies, asthmatic conditions, chronic bed-wetting, bad backs, bad eyes, and trick knees. Requests for deferment on the basis of conscientious objection were flooding draft boards. Thousands emigrated to Canada rather than serve.

In the fall of 1967 an estimated crowd of 35,000 pro-testors, including Dr. Benjamin Spock, Norman Mailer, and Robert Lowell, marched on the Pentagon at the end of a week of anti-war ferment rising across the country. The Oakland draft-induction center was surrounded by 10,000 protestors as Joan Baez sang "I'm Going to Lay Down My Green Beret." At the Boston Commons 4,000 demonstrators witnessed a draft-card burning ceremony. At Brooklyn College, 1,000 students protested against the presence of Navy recruiters. At Oberlin College, students

surrounded and trapped a Navy recruiter in his car for
several hours. Dow Chemical became a popular target on
virtually every campus.

The war protest was escalating, but the war was continuing with no end in sight. Congress eliminated deferments for graduate students rather than institute a lottery
system of draft, leading Harvard President Nathan Pusey
to say that this legislation would leave only "the lame, the
halt, the blind, and the female" in the graduate schools. A
solemn nonviolent anti-Vietnam demonstration took place
at the University of Wisconsin where mourners shuffled
past a mock cemetery of 400 white crosses in front of the
administration building, Bascom Hall. A sign read, "Bascom Memorial Cemetery, Class of 1968."

At a point in the winter of 1968 when nothing in the
System seemed to work, Eugene McCarthy declared that
he would run in the primary of New Hampshire against
President Johnson. From the beginning, McCarthy said
that his desire to give young people a reasonable alternative
to rioting and picketing was a major factor in his decision
to run. The college students responded. They responded
much more than either McCarthy or anyone else could
have predicted. As James Reston said (March 20, 1968),
"McCarthy didn't organize them [the college students] or,
at the start, even inspire them. They inspired *him* and in
some odd way, which shows that there are power and magic
in the old democratic fog even in this cynical age. They
really demonstrated—consciously and unconsciously, probably the latter—what is meant by 'the flexible and courageous' use of cooperative intelligence."

The campaign in New Hampshire was dubbed the
Children's Crusade. Student volunteers, each bringing his

own sleeping bag and typewriter, arrived by the hundreds each weekend from Smith, Mount Holyoke, Amherst, Harvard, Yale, Radcliffe, Columbia, and Barnard. Some lesser known schools such as Belknap, Rivier, and Dunbarton were represented. From more distant places—Duke and the University of Michigan—students arrived by bus or by car. *Time* magazine called them Gene McCarthy's ballot children: "In an era when many younger Americans are turning away from involvement in the democratic process, by dropping out either to psychedelia or to the nihilism of the New Left, the cool, crisply executed crusade of Gene McCarthy's ballot children provided heartening evidence that the generation gap is bridgeable—politically, at least."

The students who came out for McCarthy were anti-war and anti-L.B.J. Many had participated in the march on the Pentagon in addition to other anti-war demonstrations on and off campus. Having operated outside the political system and been frustrated, they sought change by operating within. The work was not glamorous; it was in fact as tedious and demanding in New Hampshire as it was later in other primary campaigns. The students made up mass mailing lists and rang doorbells. To escape the radical image, miniskirted girls went midi, and bearded boys either shaved or stayed in back rooms. The motto was "Get clean for Gene." Mr. Clean did exceedingly well in New Hampshire, thanks to the ballot children. And they went on to the Wisconsin primary where student volunteers poured in from Illinois, Michigan, Minnesota, and Iowa.

Part of McCarthy's personal appeal to students was his eloquence, his wit, and his restrained style, all of which helped to make him a romantic symbol. He said in a speech in Milwaukee, "No one who's insensitive to poetry and song can have respect for learning, and no one who has no respect for learning can have real respect for justice, and no one who does not respect justice can, in fact, manifest a true love for his country."

In the spring of 1968 James Reston of the *Times* (June 16, 1968) wrote, "The great adventure in the universities to transform American politics and elect a President acceptable to the young and the poor is not achieving its goals. The Old Politics and the familiar figures are prevailing over the new, but the campus movement has not failed. . . . It has demonstrated that the idealism and energy of college students, working within the system, can influence even if they cannot dominate the decisions of the parties, the candidates and the electorate. They helped bring about the withdrawal of President Johnson . . ."

The rest of the McCarthy saga is political history of a remarkable spring. Robert Kennedy declared his candidacy immediately after McCarthy's strong showing in New Hampshire; Nelson Rockefeller finally decided to enter the ring; L.B.J. withdrew from consideration for another term of office; Robert Kennedy was assassinated on the night of the primary in California. Hubert Humphrey was nominated by the Democratic convention in Chicago, which was marred by the bloodshed of hundreds of college students beaten by the Chicago police outside of the convention hall.

By late spring of 1968, student unrest was shifting from the national scene to the campus. In the week of April 23 to 30, Students for a Democratic Society (S.D.S.) and the Students Afro-American Society occupied five buildings at Columbia University with the help of 700 to 1,000 students. For the remainder of the semester, the campus was in complete chaos. The Columbia incident represented a shift in strategy that was to influence student disorder throughout the country. The radicals were turning their attention to the university. Frustrated by their failure to influence national policy by demonstrations off campus, student radicals directed their energies at a smaller and more manageable target—and one that was certainly more sympathetic and thus more vulnerable.

The Columbia uprising grew haphazardly. The three announced causes for the seizure and occupation of campus buildings were:

1. To prevent the building of a gymnasium in Morningside Park, which would take away park area from Columbia's black neighbors.
2. Opposition to the university's relationship to the Institute for Defense Analysis, which symbolized complicity in the war in Vietnam.
3. Opposition to the discipline imposed upon six S.D.S. leaders for breaking the rule against indoor demonstrations.

The report of the fact-finding commission appointed to investigate the disturbances at Columbia University, chaired by former U.S. Solicitor General, Archibald Cox, came to the conclusion that "the avowed objectives of the April demonstrations, stripped of their context and symbolism, were inadequate causes for an uprising." As symbols, however, they became very useful in the active support of moderates after the police bust in which 712 were arrested and 148 were injured. What was important at Columbia and at other institutions later was the strong evidence of sufficient student alienation to feed such an event. As the Cox Commission said (p. 190), "By its final days the revolt enjoyed both wide and deep support among the students and junior faculty and in lesser degree among the senior professors. The grievances of the rebels were felt equally by a still larger number, probably a majority, of the students. The trauma of the violence that followed police intervention intensified emotions, but support for the demonstrators rested upon broad discontent and widespread sympathy for their position."

Demonstrations concerning the war took place in numerous colleges across the country. Some took the form of orderly, peaceful student marches against recruitment on campus by interviewers representing the C.I.A., the armed forces, or private corporations, like Dow Chemical, with war contracts.

Some protesters marched on the sidewalk in front of induction centers. Sometimes the strategy was to sit or lie in the street and block the access of traffic to the induction center. In the fall of 1968, Oberlin students surrounded a Naval recruiting officer's car to prevent him from reaching his assigned office. They were driven away with tear gas and the Navy recruiter retired from the campus. A band of 75 members of the S.D.S. at Princeton University blockaded the entrance to the headquarters of the Institute for Defense Analysis with partial success. "The I.D.A. research is an integral part of the American war machine, which is presently being used in Vietnam to wage one of the most violent wars in human history," an S.D.S. spokesman declared as the blockage was being set up.

Some 250 student body presidents and college newspaper editors declared in a statement sent to President Nixon that they would refuse military induction as long as the war in Vietnam continued. They were making this choice "contrary to our respect for law," they said, because the only other alternative would be to accept induction, "which we feel would be irresponsible to ourselves, our country, and our fellow man."

A group of students at Stanford staged a nine-day sit-in at the applied electronics laboratory on the campus to demonstrate against all classified research and to end all chemical and biological warfare research and counterinsurgency studies at Stanford Research Institute in adjacent Menlo Park.

The idea of calling a one-day research halt on March 4, 1969, to dramatize the over-militarization of research was born at a dinnertable conversation of three M.I.T. physics graduate students. The idea spread, and faculty and students from an estimated thirty universities observed the one-day research halt, including Yale, Cornell, Stanford, Columbia, Rutgers, Dartmouth, Minnesota, Maryland, Northwestern, and the University of California divisions at Berkeley, Santa Cruz, and Irvine.

"Hell No, We Won't Go" was a common slogan, and draft resistance was the advice being given on many campuses. Among those who became well known in the anti-draft movement were the chaplain of Yale University, William Sloane Coffin, and the world-renowned pediatrician Dr. Benjamin Spock.

The status of the R.O.T.C. was an issue for ferment on many college campuses. Interruptions and disturbances of R.O.T.C. awards ceremonies were frequent. By 1969 the use of the R.O.T.C. issue to radicalize the campuses was quite successful.

A group of students, led by an organization called Coalition for Social Justice, staged a sit-in at the basement of the administration building at Hofstra University. They demanded the abolition of R.O.T.C. and physical education on campus. About 100 students at Boston University took possession of the quarters of the Dean of Students demanding that all university support of R.O.T.C. be dropped. Ninety state troopers were called to arrest students occupying Parkhurst Hall of Dartmouth College over the same issue. Thirty-six students served 26 days of a 30-day sentence, receiving 4 days off for good behavior. Interviewed by a *New York Times* reporter, one of the jailed students said, "It was a very enriching experience . . . We laid our bodies on the line and we felt the oppression of society directly. I feel a lot better now. I came to terms with myself and with my beliefs and I know better than ever now why I am against R.O.T.C. and the war in Vietnam."

Not everyone agreed with the campus radicals. A student-conducted poll at Brown University indicated a majority favored keeping R.O.T.C. programs on campus. Of the 1,300 students participating, 68 percent said R.O.T.C. should stay in some form, 84 percent said the opposition to the program by the S.D.S. did not reflect their opinions, and 53 percent disapproved of building seizures. A similar poll at Northeastern University also supported the continuance of R.O.T.C. A faculty vote at Tufts recommended the abolishment of R.O.T.C., but a student referendum disagreed and supported its continuance on campus—though without academic credit. As a result of protests, a number of colleges took academic credit away from R.O.T.C. courses.

The students of the Sixties felt strongly about the injustices to the black people in the ghettos and the war in Vietnam. The student movement starting early in the Sixties was focused largely on these two issues outside of the university. Students became increasingly aware, however, of the need to be included in the decision-making process if they were to be able to make any difference outside if not within the campus itself. So the issue of student power became a foremost element of the explosion taking place. The massive anonymity of the government and the unmanageability of the social system had been demonstrated to frustrated students trying to bring about change in the nation. Their anger was released as they struck out at the universities. The universities became the target for all the tension and frustration of the black ghettos and the war in Vietnam. A vague half-hope still existed in the minds of some moderates that if a university, as part of the establishment, could be politicalized, the university as an influential corporate body could then effectively lead to changes in the nation's policies.

By the late Sixties, it was difficult to be a college student and not participate in, or be affected by, some kind of "in"—sit-in, sleep-in, stand-in. A Gallup Poll estimated that 20 percent of the students participated in some kind of protest. Although the core of the radical Left represented only about 2 percent of the student population, protests took place on hundreds of campuses. Some sit-ins were ignored by administration and students alike; some "radicalized" the campus; others gained support from the student body when repressive measures were used; and some caused complete disruption of the campus. They took place from coast to coast, from small religiously affiliated colleges to state universities. The issues varied: some serious and compelling, some "unnegotiable," some arbitrary, and others purposely constructed to "bring down the establishment."

The mood of the late Sixties, particularly 1968 and 1969, was clear. From the Columbia "bust" in the spring of 1968 until the Harvard explosion in the spring of 1969 —the mood of Campus, U.S.A., was one of confrontation, escalation, and protest. The mass media played them up. The topic of student unrest consumed pages and pages of daily newspapers, *Time, Newsweek, Life, Look, Fortune Magazine, Harper's Magazine, Atlantic, The New York Review of Books,* among other.

Fortune Magazine commissioned Daniel Yankelorrick, Incorporated, an attitude-research firm, to execute a depth survey of college-educated youth between 18 to 24. They found that three-fifths of college youths were "practical-minded"—that is, they were in college because it looked like the natural route to high-paying, high-rank jobs.

The other two-fifths had a lack of concern about making money. They were most likely majoring in humanities, were vague about their career expectations, seemed interested in finding work that was intellectually challenging and somehow relevant to their social concerns. About three-fifths of this group believed it appropriate to engage in civil disobedience to further causes they supported. The *Fortune* survey suggested that behind the small and highly visible activist minority was a much larger and generally "invisible" minority of forerunners holding similar dissident attitudes, which formed a universe of some 2,300,000 activists.

Whether or not a so-called "average" student, not terribly alienated from society or his parents, could completely ignore "the scene" if not "the Movement" was made doubly difficult by the exposure that media gave to these events. Nevertheless, the need for a sense of commitment, accomplishment, and making a difference, of forcing change, should not be underestimated. Although only a small percentage of the students wanted a revolution in American society, a substantial number of the students were concerned about injustices in the world and in the United States. They were concerned about the war in Vietnam, racial tokenism, and the lack of student involvement in the process of American higher education. They did care, and that distinguished them from the Silent Generation of the Fifties.

Internal collegiate matters were one source of contention. Southern Illinois students demanded student control of the campus newspaper and radio station in addition to a larger voice in university affairs and attempted to take over the president's office. The students at State University College at Geneseo, who were demanding a stronger voice in curriculum, faculty slection, policies, and dormitory rules, staged nightly sit-ins at the College Center for more than a week. A hundred students demonstrated at the University of Oregon to demand a voice on the selection committee of the new university president, and as a result three students were put on the committee. Princeton undergraduates massed outside the administration building to make demands that included a call for eventual turnover of power from trustees to students and faculty members.

Some 700 Marietta College students, many carry replicas of the Revolutionary War "Don't Tread On Me" flag, staged a three-block silent protest march. The demonstration, ending a two-day student class boycott, was in protest over the expulsion of the student body president-elect, Earle J. Maiman of Scranton, Pennsylvania, for "inflammatory remarks." In addition, an estimated 100 of the demonstrators participated in a hunger strike that organizers said would continue until the issue of Maiman's expulsion was resolved. At the University of Denver, when a sit-in for "student rights" was attempted in the registrar's office, prompt action was the answer. Police were called in and 40 demonstrators were arrested and expelled on the spot.

Protests against the non-renewal of contracts or refusal

to grant tenure to popular professors was common. Police arrested 24 students at Roosevelt University when they protested the university's decision not to rehire Staughton Lynd. At New York University, 100 students seized the Hall of Languages to protest a decision not to renew the contract of a popular young English instructor, before leaving under threat of court order. Students occupied the University of Chicago administration building for 16 days before they conceded that the demonstration had failed in its efforts to have the university rehire an assistant professor.

Not all colleges, however, are out for the same thing. At Pikesville College in Kentucky, student dissidents were protesting long-haired professors, women teachers in miniskirts, and a liberal president who wanted to give students more freedom and make the curriculum more relevant.

About 3,000 Georgia Tech students broke with the current trend in campus demonstrations and staged their own version, one honoring the retiring Tech president, Edwin Harrison.

They called it "Wonderful Ed's Day," and appropriated a 10-foot high letter "T" off the schools' administration building to present to him as a going-away present. The school paper reported:

Of the nearly 3,000 college presidents in this country, I guess I am the only one that's being given a demonstration of this kind, the 53-year old Mr. Harrison said when a band of long-haired musicians gave up their "psychedelic" offerings long enough for him to be heard.

And so it was that hundreds of demonstrations took place on campuses across the country. But finally it took place at a campus "where it couldn't happen"—Harvard.

On April 9, 1969, about 70 members of S.D.S. entered the administration building at Harvard and ushered out, more or less gracefully, all its occupants including the deans. After an afternoon and an evening of deliberation, the officials of Harvard decided to call the police. At 4:45 A.M. the Cambridge police and six buses of state troopers entered Harvard Yard to clear University Hall. A total of 196 persons were arrested, heads were cracked, and 48 persons including 5 policemen had to be given hospital treatment. Harvard had had its "bust." Before the spring semester ended, the faculty had rebuked their dean and their president for calling in the police; 10,000 members of the Harvard community had gathered at Soldiers Field, Harvard's colonnaded football stadium, to consider the issues and decide upon a course of action; the Afro-American group presented their demands for establishing a new department for Afro-American studies with black students as full voting members on the faculty committee; and finally Harvard removed academic credit for R.O.T.C.

It became increasingly difficult for the public to keep the events of campus disorder in perspective. The sheer number of campus demonstrations, strikes, and sit-ins reported in the press and on television was bewildering. Even the sedate *New York Times* ran a front-page box summary entitled "Campus Unrest in Brief." A backlash directed to all campus protests developed quickly.

Both houses of Congress held hearings and investigations on campus unrest. S.D.S. was singled out by some legislators as a subversive organization dedicated to the overthrow of the country. The House Internal Security Committee (formerly the House Un-American Activities Committee) began to subpoena individual student records. The repressive forces of an enraged public were moving.

State legislators introduced and passed bills designed to punish campus disrupters by jail, expulsion, or forfeiture of scholarship aid. In California alone, over seventy bills were introduced.

Reaction to the disruption began also to set in among the less than radical students. Counter-movements by the conservative organization Young Americans for Freedom sprang up at several campuses. At Michigan State University more than 10,000 students signed petitions condemning "intimidation, violence, and disruption" on the campus. The "silent majority" was starting to collect signatures to petition for order at San Francisco State, Mankato State College (Minnesota), and other places.

At Franklin and Marshall College, editors of the student newspaper urged a national coalition of "non-revolutionary radicals, liberals, and moderates to quickly isolate and defeat the disruptive radicals." In an editorial, the students said, "The fact is that the lure of campus destructionists to draw fellow students to their purposes is getting weaker. The reform-by-violence movement is doomed and the radicals know it."

A bill pending in the House Education and Labor Committee would have cut off Federal aid to colleges and universities that failed to submit a detailed plan for maintaining order. The Nixon Administration was finally persuaded to stop such repressive action by the Federal government. Opposition to such legislation came from several quarters, including the American Civil Liberties Union and the National Commission on the Causes and Prevention of Violence.

The A.C.L.U. statement said, in part:

We believe in the right and are committed to the protection of all peaceful, non-obstructive forms of protest, including mass demonstration, picketing, rallies and other dramatic forms. However, we are deeply disturbed about some methods that some student activists have used in the attempt to achieve their ends; methods which violate and subvert the basic principles of freedom of expression and academic freedom. Protest that deprives others of the opportunity to speak or be heard, or that requires physical take-over of buildings to disrupt the educational process, or the incarceration of administrators and others are anti-civil-libertarian and incompatible with the nature and high purpose of an educational institution.

As to the bills that were being considered in Congress and in state legislatures to curb campus violence, the A.C.L.U. statement said, "We are opposed to these measures. Their imposition is not likely to quiet down but rather to inflame further the unrest. Many of them are vague and would superimpose severe financial penalties in addition to punishment already provided by law. Their thrust often would be effective only against the poor. What is more, they threaten the traditional autonomy of academic communities to govern themselves."

Of the 2,500 colleges and universities in the United States, scarcely two dozen were seriously disrupted. Of the 6,700,000 college students (over 4 million full-time), perhaps only 2 percent can be considered radical. But the events of the Sixties affected far more colleges and many more individuals than those bare statistics would indicate. It was more than just the media that frequently magnified incidents because of the insatiable public appetite for such news. Perhaps it was simply the impact of seeing many of the best students at the best institutions—to use Jack Newfield's phrase, "the prophetic minority"—viewing the world, the country, and their colleges from a radically different perspective and proposing radical solutions to societal problems and utilizing radically new political tactics. The mood of the Sixties, particularly the late Sixties, had a profound effect on all students in college, for better or for worse.

CHAPTER VIII

THE BLACK STUDENT

In the Sixties it was important, terribly important, to do your own thing. Black students were no different. They wanted their own movement, their own identity. The murder of Martin Luther King, Jr., in early 1968 and the long explosive summers in most of the major urban centers alarmed the country. The separatist political movement off campus, led by Stokeley Carmichael, Rap Brown, and others, began to move onto the campus. The result was a mixture of confusion, belligerence, and disagreement not only between black and white, but among blacks.

King's assassination signaled the drive to establish Afro-American history courses and Afro-American majors, to increase the number of black professors, and to enroll greater numbers of black students. The black students' take-over at Boston University—the institution where King earned his doctorate—was only one of such sit-ins throughout the country.

Several weeks after King's assassination, a group of black students took possession of the administration building at Boston University. Converging on the four-story building at 8 A.M., they escorted out a handful of university employees who had reported for work. Then they chained the four entrance doors to the building, and said that they would remain until their nineteen demands were met.

President Arland F. Christ-Janer entered for a talk with the black students. They proposed that the Theology Building be named after Dr. King. They urged the establishment of an Afro-American Coordinating Center at the University. They proposed a "talent bank" of experts from whom Negro business organizations could seek advice on economics, legal matters, and urban development. They wanted more Negro students to be admitted the following fall, more Negro faculty members, and courses in Negro history.

The demands were similar to those at other institutions throughout the country, and both faculty and administration responded favorably to the desires of the black students.

However, not all these confrontations were so easily resolved. By the fall of 1968, San Francisco State College, long recognized as one of the best state colleges in the California system, was shut down because of the racial tension on campus. The tension had begun a year previously when Black Student Union members wrecked the offices of the student paper and beat several staff members for printing what the blacks called racial slurs. Five Black Student Union members were suspended. And when the demands for immediate reinstatement of these students were refused, students held a sit-in at the administration building. The matter became a political issue in California, and the regents interrogated the college's president, John Summerskill, in a televised inquisition. Summerskill resigned after only twenty-one months in office.

In the fall of 1968, new demonstrations by B.S.U. members and the S.D.S. were stirred up as a result of the suspension of twenty-two-year-old George Murray, a part-time teacher who was also minister of education for the Black Panthers. Underlying the Murray issue was a demand by black militants for unrestricted admission of black students and a separate black-studies department. Murray urged students to "kill all the slave masters," among whom he counted President Johnson, Chief Justice Warren, and Governor Reagan. He told students at San Francisco State to bring guns on campus for "self-defense." The order to suspend Murray apparently came from State College Chancellor Glenn S. Dumke to the new president, Robert Smith. What developed on the campus of 16,300 white students and 800 blacks was a strike called by black militants in which fires were set in various buildings, equipment was ruined, and laboratories destroyed. The San Francisco tactical police squad was summoned and the outbreaks of savage violence between students and police finally forced the college to be closed down for a month.

President Smith, another victim of student rebellion, also resigned, and Dr. Samuel I. Hayakawa was appointed acting president of the strife-torn college. Hayakawa, a nationally known semanticist, immediately reopened the college with the help of 600 policemen, but not without bloodshed and mass arrests.

Student rebellions supporting the demands of black students affected at least six other colleges in northern California: San Mateo, Vallejo, San José, Sacramento, Chico, and Fresno. Farther south, at San Fernando Valley State College the police clashed with 2,000 demonstrators and arrested nearly 300.

The establishment of an independent black-studies department remained a problem not only at San Francisco State but also at other institutions, including Harvard. If black militants had their way, few if any whites would be involved. On several campuses the black students demanded the right to hire and fire teachers in the black-studies department. At Harvard, the faculty voted to give black students a voting voice in the appointment of professors and the formulation of a new program in Afro-American studies. Similar demands were heard around the country.

"The danger is that white students will flood Black Studies courses," said Dr. Nathan Hare, the fiery black militant who was briefly the director of the Black Studies Department at San Francisco State College. "It may be necessary eventually to distinguish black education for blacks and black education for whites."

Black students at Brandeis University, a private institution founded and largely supported by the Jewish community, unexpectedly occupied the communications building for eleven days. President Morris Abrams deplored their action as one that came "without prior complaint." Nevertheless he met with representatives of the black students and agreed to most of their demands for greater black representation in the student body and more courses on black history and culture.

Black and Puerto Rican students at Queens College in New York City demanded the right to control the appointment of the director of SEEK (Search for Education, Elevation and Knowledge) program that was set up in 1966 to help minority students. The 26,000-student campus had to be shut down for two days in January "to avoid possible violence."

The beginning of the spring semester of 1969 brought with it a new wave of confrontations and demands by black students and their white sympathizers: more black students, black professors, and courses on black history and culture; a voice for students in the hiring and firing of faculty for black studies; and black dormitories and other facilities.

At the University of Wisconsin, where there were about 500 undergraduate black students among the student body of 34,000, demands were made to make studies for black students more "relevant." The blacks had the support of the Wisconsin Student Association as well as twenty-three other campus organizations. In a week-long symposium on the "black revolution," militant Negroes predominated among the speakers. Nathan Hare of San Francisco State College said the University of Wisconsin needed a revolution to contest its white middle-class orientation.

Student strife at Wisconsin disrupted classes for three days. Demonstrators who tried to prevent students from entering classroom buildings were challenged by student members of the right-wing Young Americans for Freedom. The counter-demonstrators wore "H" armbands to identify themselves with Dr. S. I. Hayakawa, former University of Wisconsin student and teacher now heading San Francisco State College.

Before it finally ended, Governor Knowles had called up first 900 National Guardsmen, then an additional 1,000, as students responded by turning out in far larger numbers than before in support of the demonstrators. An estimated 5,000 students joined in a rally after the Guard arrived on campus. Bayonets, clubs, and tear gas were used by Guardsmen and the police before the strike ended.

Even white universities in the South experienced such confrontations. Following King's assassination, a four-day silent vigil and boycotting of classes took place at Duke University. Among the demands made were higher wages for non-academic employees, recognition of a union of non-academic employees, and the resignation of President Douglas Knight from the segregated Hope Valley Country Club. In the spring of 1969, seventy members of the Afro-American Society seized the ground floor of the administration building and named it the "Malcolm X Liberation School." The demonstration was to demand a black-studies program at Duke where there were approximately 100 black students in a student body of 8,000. Before the crisis ended, a brawl erupted between the police, the black students, and an estimated 1,000 white student supporters. Duke University finally agreed to the establishment of a black-studies program, the first to be set up at a major Southern university. The college also agreed to black insistence upon a separate dormitory for black students and their own adviser—in apparent reversal of the usual demand for integration in the schools.

Protests for black studies or increase in enrollment of black students did not escape the smaller colleges. More than eighty Negro students and teachers occupied a classroom building at Wesleyan University for twelve hours to protest the faculty's refusal to cancel classes for Malcolm X Day. Bowdoin College with a total student body of 950, of which 20 are black, established an Afro-American major. Forty members of the Association of Black Collegians at Colgate University seized the faculty club to press their demands for an Afro-American Center. A four-day sit-in of 33 black women students at Vassar gained a minor in black studies, hiring of black teachers, and a black cooperative in a dormitory. Even the normally calm campuses like Upsala and Iona were faced with lists of black student demands.

These demands were not aimed exclusively at white institutions. Protests also took place where students were predominantly Negro. Stillman College was closed briefly after a four-day student boycott in protest of various conditions at the school. Cheyney State College in Pennsylvania was shut down for a week during a mass student demonstration demanding more policy-making involvement by students. The National Guard was called in at Wilberforce in Ohio to quell the riots. Protesting Negro students at

Atlanta University chained shut the door of a room where the school's board of trustees was meeting, to demonstrate their demands for the resignation of eighteen trustees and the merger of the six-college university complex into one school to be renamed Dr. Martin Luther King University. Hampton Institute in Virginia was closed after approximately eighty to one hundred students moved into the administration building following a mass meeting during which 700 students agreed to boycott classes.

At Southern University, in Baton Rouge, Louisiana, where student demands included a black-studies department, a course in black liberation, and improvements in the physical structure of the campus, the police and students exchanged gunfire in a shower of firebombs, tear gas, rocks, and bottles. Howard University, the nation's largest predominantly Negro university, was closed after the seizure of buildings by militant students and non-students in the spring of 1968 over the issue of black power, and again in spring, 1969, when the issues were: student power, student participation in teacher evaluation, curriculum reform, and de-emphasis of final examinations.

It was the front-page photographs, nationally displayed, of armed black students leaving Cornell University's student center after a thirty-six-hour occupation that symbolized the atmosphere of tension. Several professors resigned over the bitter debate as to whether the students should be given amnesty.

The Afro-American members said they had seized Straight Hall to dramatize their concern over the design of a black-studies program, their anger over the judicial reprimands against three black students the previous day, and fear for their physical safety on the campus and in the Ithaca area. They contended that Cornell's 250 black students had been subjected to repeated threats and harassing telephone calls. A cross had been burned the previous night on the lawn of a black women's cooperative residence on the campus.

"I wonder how many people in this room can conceive of what a burning cross means to black people," the Black Liberation Front spokesman, Tom Jones, told an assembly of white students and faculty members the following week. "That has always been a symbol, in the black experience, that we're going to be killed, we're going to be raped, we're going to be arrested, we're going to be castrated," he said.

The incident began shortly before dawn on Saturday, April 19th, when about 100 Negro militants entered Willard Straight Hall, the student union, routed a number of visiting parents from their beds, and seized the building. That night they armed themselves with shotguns and rifles. Their specific grievance was the action of a newly created faculty-student disciplinary board against five leaders of a series of demonstrations demanding a separate "black college" within the university (three had been reprimanded and two acquitted). On Sunday, Dean of Faculty Robert D. Miller agreed to ask the faculty to "nullify" the board's action, and the students evacuated the building. On Monday, however, the faculty voted to reject the nullification. Mass demonstrations by black and white students followed, and one Negro student leader went on the radio to warn: "Cornell has three hours to live."

Before the faculty met again, an aroused student body of liberals and moderates—about 2,000—sat through the night on a basketball court to show their support for amnesty for the black students. The editorial in the school newspaper, *The Cornell Daily Sun,* said, "The huge congregation . . . serves notice to the faculty that it has had enough of pigheadedness and insensitivity . . . Cornell was headed for an explosion and the faculty didn't seem to care enough to avoid it. The thousands in Barton Hall last night did care."

When the faculty met again, it reversed itself and finally agreed to ratify the agreement between members of the Afro-American Society and the Dean of Faculty. The damage, however, had been done. The backlash that had been developing all spring found a focus in the Cornell incident. Denunciation of what was considered "capitulation and appeasement" of students in general and blacks in particular came loudly and clearly in Congress, state capitols, and from alumni.

A still more acute level of campus turmoil was reached as blacks battled whites at City College of New York. Blacks and Puerto Ricans forced several campuses of City University to close over the issue of the open admission of non-white students regardless of their level of college preparation. The issue of backlash, which had been generally considered as reaction by off-campus forces, now added a new dimension: counterforce from within the schools.

CHAPTER IX

THE MOVEMENT OF THE LATE SIXTIES

THE Movement was many, many things. No organization, no individual, and no particular ideology had a monopoly on it. The Movement was leaderless, but forceful. It was a mood, perhaps, more than anything else.

The Movement was not the exclusive province of any particular branch of the New Left. S.D.S. was no doubt influential with the ideals expressed in their charter known as the Port Huron statement, as well as the organization of local chapters to bring down the universities if not the Establishment. But, the Movement included those college students who joined the Peace Corps, VISTA, or participated in the Freedom Ride to Jackson and helped to register Negroes in the South. It had included also many students who tutored slum children, protested against the Bomb, burned draft cards, and marched on the Pentagon. It certainly had to include persons who participated in the Student Nonviolent Coordinating Committee (SNCC) as well as the activists in the Free Speech Movement at Berkeley. The Movement included community organizers in city slums and helpers of the striking farm workers in San Joaquin Valley.

The Movement, then, included more than the memberships of young radical organizations. What it encompassed (and still encompasses) depended upon those thousands or hundreds of thousands of students who joined in the various causes, events, and demonstrations in the Sixties. As Professors Paul Jacobs and Saul Landau said:

> The leitmotifs that dominate the Movement extend far beyond politics. The Movement is much more than anti-Vietnam marches, civil rights demonstrations, and student sit-ins. To be in the Movement is to search for a psychic community, in which one's own identity can be defined, social and personal relationships based on love can be established and can grow, unfettered by the cramping pressures of the careers and life styles so characteristic of America today.
>
> The Movement rejects the careers and life styles of the American liberal, too, for to the Movement it is the liberal way of life and frame of mind that represents the evil of America. Those in the Movement feel that modern American liberals have substituted empty rhetoric for significant content, obscured the principles of justice by administrative bureaucracy, sacrificed human values for efficiency, and hypocritically justified a brutal attempt to establish American hegemony over the world with sterile anti-Communism.

The Movement was also a matter of style and culture. This student editorial was written at Boston University in the spring of 1969:

> What SDS sees as the Movement passed away with McCarthy Politics and political movements are dead as effective means for revolutionary change, and in America at least, so is violent revolution. What the real Movement consists of is not the committed, not the American Liberation Front, not soldiers in the revolutionary army, but simply the alienated and the disenfranchised.
>
> But the Movement is in actuality only the illusion of a movement. It is not politics, but theatre. It exists only because the mass media exist. It is dramatics, theatre, propaganda. It is Abbie

Hoffman with FUCK on his forehead, Jerry Rubin with a plastic machinegun, the Fathers Berrigan pouring duck blood over draft files, Martin Luther King at the head of the Selma march, a half-million people parading in the streets of New York, the Black Panthers armed to the teeth in the California State House. It is Country Joe and the Fish singing "Super Bird," Jim Morrison screaming about revolution while he takes some clothes off, Father Groppi Blacks into the white suburbs of Milwaukee, the Yippies taking over Grand Central Station. It is a teenager flashing a moon at MacDonald's.

The Movement is not a united grassroots consciousness. It is Ungerer's posters, Feiffer's cartoons, Crumb's comics, LeRoi Jones' poems, Jimi Hendrix' guitar, Owsley's acid, everybody's grass. The Movement is nothing but the theatrics of leaders, but theatre in most forms is more effective than dialectics. The leaders lead by example only. One looks, listens, becomes. Only the ideologues follow.

The SDS "educational approach" will never really succeed because America's youth are children of television and not students of dialectic. For the TV Generation, the Medium is Movement. SDS has failed to grasp fully the lesson of Chicago, that America can only be moved by mass psychological terrorism inflicted by and through its media. The actors in the Theatre of Movement must manipulate the media, must make a point theatrically before the largest audience possible. TV coverage of Vietnam War, of the Battle of Chicago, of the ghetto rebellions, of the murder of Robert Kennedy has electrified and motivated a stupid and lethargic mass-America, and the Beatles, Stones, Doors, and Fish have given it a new definition of personal freedom.

What is needed then is not more Herbert Marcuse but more Norman Mailer. Marcuse can explain just what it is that's happening to any Mr. Jones who cares to listen, but ideologies are politics, and politics are dead. Sidewalk chats are nice in the springtime, but change will be brought on by constant confrontation: Building take-over, marches, looting, pop music, TV news programs, turned in draft cards, long hair, drugs, obscenity, shock and guerilla theatre.

The hippies popularized a new word, *psychedelic,* which the Random House Dictionary defined as: "Of or noting a mental state of great calm, intensely pleasureful perception of the senses, esthetic entrancement, and creative impetus; of or noting any of the group of drugs producing this effect." Hallucinogenic, or mind-expanding, or mind manifesting drugs range from the mild ones that include marijuana to the much more potent LSD. Acid heads have described "trips" with "fantastic visions of extraordinary vividness accompanied by a kaleidoscopic play of intense coloration."

The Food and Drug Administration estimated that tens of thousands of college students have tried LSD and several times that number have used marijuana. With these drugs have come a psychedelic philosophy, culture, and art. It is expressed in heightened perceptions in sight and sound and distortions of the senses. When it was discovered that LSD could not only cause psychotic illnesses but also possibly that it could alter human chromosomes, use of acid began to decline.

If LSD was not too common on the campuses, marijuana (pot, grass) was. Thirteen midshipmen at Annapolis admitted to smoking marijuana and were dismissed. Psychiatrist Seymour Halleck declared at a meeting of the American Psychiatric Association that "smoking marijuana has become almost an emblem of alienation. The alienated student realizes that the use of 'pot' mortifies his parents and enrages authorities." The Harvard *Crimson* estimated that 25 percent of the students had smoked pot at least once.

Undercover agents, sometimes detectives in disguise and sometimes students hired by the police, spied on campuses to get leads on the sale of drugs. State University of New York at Stony Brook was raided twice with what students called "Gestapo tactics." Generally the students' opinion, shared by many professors, was that pot is harmless, not habit forming, and should be legalized. The debate had by no means ended by the close of the Sixties, for campus culture had been taken over by psychedelic colors, designs, and music.

At shops in San Francisco, Los Angeles, and New York, psychedelic paraphernalia included prism spectacles and kaleidoscopes at first probably intended to give vicarious acid heads a hint of what a trip might be like, and became a general rage, even among younger high school students. The Beatles song "Lucy in the Sky with Diamonds" was instantly understood as a code for LSD. When the Beatles sang of taking "Lovely Rita" (meter maid) out to tea, kids immediately thought "marijuana" not "orange pekoe." "The Magic Carpet Ride" and the Beatles "Yellow Submarine" were both metaphorical for a drug trip.

Robert Gorham Davis wrote in *The New York Times Book Review,* June 29, 1969:

Nowadays the young, when they want art that seems to them alive, do not naturally choose words on the printed page. Their culture is aural, visual, tactile. They prefer theater, particularly the theater of cruelty, to reading a novel. And they prefer films to the theater—films like those of Godard, where the words are absurd or banal, and the image is everything.

The extracurricular interests in the arts reflected a shift in the tastes of American college students. *The New York Times* reported, May 19, 1969:

They are reading more books than ever, but films stir them ever so much more. They have made poetry thrive—as something to hear, rather than as something to read. They would rather create for themselves than have someone create for them. They are more passionate about intent than about form. They want art to function as either pure emotional pleasure or social tool."

Film was undoubtedly the most popular of the art forms as a staple pastime. Students consumed anything that was nearby and convenient, including Hollywood spectaculars. Many of these, by 1969, were being created by new young producers, directors, and actors who were supposed to know what appealed to the young. It was not enough to have Richard Burton and Elizabeth Taylor perform Edward Albee's savage "college" scene in *Who's Afraid of Virginia Wolfe*. Bonnie and Clyde (1967) were hero and heroine of the anti-Establishment youth. *The Graduate* (1968) captured all prizes, with two new young actors. Antonioni's *Blow-Up* (1967), conveying the reality of illusion, became the greatest foreign film success, followed by the Beatles psychedelic *Yellow Submarine* in 1969. By 1969, Hollywood was fighting the low-budget maverick producer-directors "underground" films that were shown in independent theaters near the campuses. But students particularly enjoyed the older films—the W. C. Fields's and old Bogart's—and contemporary foreign films. Quite a bit of film-making was being done by college students themselves. They were extraordinarily visual minded, and the so-called "underground films" were often made with campus facilities. These were the new social documentaries.

The audio was even more prevalent. There were few college students who didn't have a guitar, electronic guitar, hi-fi set, tape recorder, or easy access to one of them. Overwhelmingly, records and tapes were the contemporary musical idiom—folk, country and western music, folk rock, soul, and rock. Groups and individuals sprang into universal fame—Arlo Guthrie, Aretha Franklin, the Mamas and the Papas, and a host of others. The music of the late Sixties reflected the mood of the Movement. Folk rock inspired participation. As one student wrote:

Rock music must not be seen apart from the movement among young people to reshape their lives in ways reflecting their intense disenchantment with societies that seem to thrive on driving people apart from each other and from all but the most vapid, romantic notions of love. As such it is a profoundly political form of music, one that opts for a different for of social organization, one that lets people love rather than makes them go to war, lets them accept the chaos and see uncertainty as a legitimate and understandable part of life.

Rock music was born of a revolt against the sham of Western culture: it was direct and gutsy and spoke to the senses. There was also a message in lyrics which attacked the war, middle-class values (even the P.T.A.), among other things. John Lennon of the Beatles said, "All our songs are anti-war." A line in Dylan's "Subterranean Home-sick Blues" goes, "Don't follow leaders." Joan Baez announced the next number with, "This one is dedicated to President Johnson and his marvelous foreign policy." Then she sang a rock and roll hit by the Supremes, "Stop! in the Name of Love."

Like the Movement, rock music and the Beatles in particular exemplified a distrust of authority, disdain for conventions, and impatience with hypocrisy.

The most astounding and unexpected musical event of the decade was the Woodstock Rock Festival to which 300,000 young people came, gathering peacefully in open fields, without preparation of food or facilities. They were all there—the hippies, the musicians, the students both high school and college, the pot smokers, the young teachers.

The "in" book on campus in the latter part of the Sixties was *Lord of the Rings* by J. R. R. Tolkien, the most popular seller since the paperback edition of *Lord of the Flies* in the early Sixties. *Rings* was a fairytale for adults with the hobbit Frodo Baggins, a three-foot high creature with long curly hair on his feet, as the hero. Hobbits are far more humane than warlike humans and other evil beings. The trends for unassigned reading on campus included books on black social problems such as *Soul on Ice* by Eldridge Cleaver, *Black Rage* by William H. Brier and Price M. Cobbs, *The Autobiography of Malcolm X,* and The Report of the National Advisory Commission on Civil Disorders.

Best-selling books on campus in the late Sixties included writings critical of the Establishment such as *Essays on Liberation* by Herbert Marcuse, or books that reject society and its conventions like Herman Hesse's *Siddhartha,* or satire on war like Joseph Heller's *Catch-22*. To understand themselves and influences around them, extracurricular reading included *The Art of Loving* by Erich Fromm and *Understanding Media* by Marshall McLuhan.

Among the students' favored contemporary fiction writers were Roth, Wolfe, Updike, Malamud, and Bellows.

By 1965 Supreme Court rulings on obscenity freed book and magazine publishers of the worst terrors of censorship. Leading literary figures lost their constraint. Mary McCarthy's *The Group* (of Vassar girls twenty years later) became pale before Philip Roth's *Portnoy's Complaint* (1969). Tom Wolfe's *The Electric Kool-Aid Acid Test* set a psychedelic pace for fiction (1967). Norman Mailer's account of the massive Washington anti-war demonstration of October 1967, *The Armies of the Night,* won both the National Book Award and the Pulitzer Prize in 1969. The 21-year-old James S. Kunen's book about the Columbia bust, *The Strawberry Statement,* captured national attention as the voice of the self-styled "revolutionary."

Poetry had a revival favoring Allen Ginsberg, e. e. cummings, and Lawrence Ferlinghetti. Science-fiction writers like Ray Bradbury, Rod Serling, Arthur C. Clarke, Robert Heinlein, and Isaac Asimov were extremely popular. Clarke combined talents with marvels of sound and light projected by producer Stanley Kubrick and theories of McLuhan to produce *2001: A Space Odyssey,* the film triumph of 1968.

Titles in the occult, astrology, and witchcraft proved to be a surprising new demand. It was difficult to decide how much of the occult rage was put on and how much was serious. *The I Ching,* a book presenting an ancient Chinese divination device that enables one to make decisions, was among the best sellers on campus. Ouija boards, which some older alumni might remember, were very popular. Meditation, Yoga, and Zen were seriously studied. An article in *The New York Times Magazine* (June 1, 1969) reported: "A certain Catholic university discovered that it had a coven of warlocks on campus (warlocks, for the uninitiated, are male witches)." As the dean of the institution put it, "We've really become progressive around here. A couple of hundred years ago we would have burned them at the stake. Twenty-five years ago I would have expelled them. Now we simply send them all to psychiatrists."

Horoscopes and books on astrology, mysticism, and magic were best sellers. Students were on the Yang-yin macrobiotic (brown rice) diet, and many were on drugs.

There were other follies. A best-selling camp classic in the middle Sixties was *Quotations from Chairman Mao Tse-tung,* which came encased in red plastic with a red ribbon marker for one dollar. Mao's sayings became as popular as the old Confucius-say. Dormitory walls were covered with posters depicting heroes and anti-heroes. Among the favorites were Chairman Mao, Allen Ginsberg in his Uncle Sam Suit, Humphrey Bogart, and Dracula. The movie *Bonnie and Clyde* stimulated a gangster-look rage on campuses that included striped double-breasted suits, wide wild neckties, brown and white shoes, and any old taxi driver hat.

For those who didn't go barefooted around campus (including to class) the "in" thing was not to wear socks. Going sockless was to the "preppy-clubby" set what the sleeveless sweatshirt was to the athletic crowd. At Columbia, students went on Manhattan theater dates sockless. The whole idea was "coolness"—a studied but very complete nonchalance.

In 1968, it was Nehru or Mao jackets with chain necklaces, often with the peace symbol as a pendant. In 1969, metal chain belts came in, for both sexes. All kinds of jackets and vests, with hippie-like appearance, have been in vogue. For young men, fringed buckskin jackets, bell-bottom trousers, capes, old military coats, old 1920 raccoon coats, and new fur jackets were "in" in 1969. Most recently Indian headbands and beads appeared with whatever else was worn. Girls still like miniskirts, especially with maxicoats. Both sexes wear every kind of pants. Any month will produce variations.

Occasionally even in the Sixties, there were pranks reminiscent of former eras. One classic took place on August 11, 1966. The Antioch College *Record* published the news the next day:

Hellish Joke Makes Dorms Inferno

In one of the most elaborate practical jokes in recent Antioch history, name plaques on 8 of the 9 halls of the Presidents dorm complex were replaced, PBX housing directories were completely revised in accordance with the new names, and even the official boards in the housing office were altered—all early Thursday morning.

The operation was executed between 2 and 4 A.M. Thusday by about 15 upperclassmen and freshmen organized into 9 squads, a source told the *Record*.

The pranksters replaced the original plastic name plaques with similar ones, bearing names alluding to hell, taken either from mythology or from Dante's *Divine Comedy*. The new names are Acheron, Dis, Naraka, Styx, Hades, Tartarus, Nastrond, and Gehenna.

Maples, the college fire department, and the only college dormitory in the complex not named for an early president of Antioch, was not renamed. A cedar gate at the corner of North College and Livermore Streets identifies the dormitory complex as "The Inferno," and warns: "Lasciate ogni speranza voi che entrate"—abandon all hope ye who enter here.

Others in the community soon became aware of the changes instituted by the anonymous group that calls itself "Renamecil (hall renaming council)."

Students found that revised PBX housing directories were issued to every dorm on campus. The new listings contained notices stating that the project had been "undertaken to provide hall names which are more masculine sounding, similar to the halls in South."

In the Union mimeographed letters from Renamecil, "a group rising from the common core of Antioch humanity," hailed its operation as one that, hopefully, would "place 'B' division of 1966 in the annals of Antioch history for all time. . . ."

Director of housing Jean Janis called it the "best practical joke since the 'Greak Auk'," which left mysterious footprints on walls, roofs, inside locked offices, and even inside the college safe. . . . The whole operation was executed in only two hours by squads working with remarkable organization and efficiency, the *Record*'s informant said.

Throughout Thursday, petitions appeared in the renamed complex and in the Union seeking community support for keeping the new names.

College life just has to be different from the good old days when a girl can attend Yale and a boy can attend Vassar! As incredible as this movement sounded to old alumni, a major breakthrough took place in the late Sixties. The male enclaves such as Yale, Wesleyan, and Princeton scrambled for a mix of women. Female bastions such as Vassar, Mount Holyoke, Skidmore, and Sarah Lawrence scrambled for a mix of men.

Separate-sex college education became increasingly anachronistic in the Sixties, as less and less distinction between the sexes occurred in professional and social life.

The announcement that the trustees of Yale and Vassar were considering a merger set the academic world, not to mention their alumni, twittering. But newspapers really had fun shortly thereafter when Vassar broke the engagement in order, as it was so delicately put, to "remain mistress in her own house," with men of her own. Or as *Time* magazine put it (October 11, 1968), "It is a woman's right to be fickle about whom she will embrace."

President Kingman Brewster recommended to the faculty that Yale admit 500 women in 1969 and thus proceed to coeducation "with style, dignity, and decisiveness." *The Yale Daily News* complained of the president's "fussiness" in wanting to describe carefully in admissions literature how women would be housed. "For 267 years," an editorial noted, "male students have been unhesitatingly entering Yale without this information."

The traditions of Princeton's famed eating clubs, described warmly by F. Scott Fitzgerald in *This Side of Paradise* in 1917, were threatened by the impending co-education program to begin at Princeton. There was the expected outcry from some alumni. One alumnus asserted, "... a basic requirement for admission ... should certainly be a burning desire ... to be a Princeton man. He should have decided that he wants to spend four years at Princeton, not Princeton with girls, or Princeton without clubs or any other Princeton. If he doesn't feel that way, he should go elsewhere. He will be happier and we will be better off without him."

Saint Xavier College, a Roman Catholic institution in Chicago, opened its doors to men for the first time in 1969. Hamilton College opened Kirkland College as a coordinate college for women. Union College in Schenectady, Franklin and Marshall, Kenyon, The University of the South, and Georgetown University were among the male institutions making plans to admit females. Sarah Lawrence and Bennington started to add men gradually, and Connecticut College also followed the trend.

Joe College is dying. Freshmen hazing and beanies are out. Fraternities, intercollegiate athletics, clubs, dances, the traditional focuses for school spirit, are fading at one speed or another.

After a long and careful study, Amherst abolished their long tradition of a strong fraternity-based social life. The report urged a shift to more broadly based residential societies to "wean students into more mature forms of independent expression." Princeton's famous eating club "Bicker" underwent a very thorough overhaul in an attempt to cut out the social stratification of the campus on social, financial, and ethnic bases. Some fraternities had to leave campuses because their national chapters, very often dominated by older alumni, refused to exclude clauses preventing minority groups from joining.

The student entering college in the Sixties was a much more sophisticated youngster who was not likely to be willing to put up with fraternity hazing, which at one time banded older alumni together. Furthermore, the social advantages of belonging to a fraternity, the opportunity to drink or to entertain girls are more widely available about the campus as parietal rules in university dormitories are liberalized.

Some college traditions remain, but the traditional "rah-rah" is hard to find. The "Big Ten," the big Southern schools, and several in the Far West maintain what can be called big-time football to sold-out stadiums. Smaller schools, particularly in the East, are struggling to keep football because of the lack of interest in this Saturday afternoon activity. Not only are the stadiums unfilled, but the football player who can maintain a satisfactory scholastic record and also devote himself to the rigors of football practice and training is hard to come by. Many carefully recruited athletes soon drop out of sports to devote themselves to studies and other activities.

Loyalty to an institution is not particularly part of this generation. One-fourth of every graduating class began school in another college. A high percentage switch and drop out before graduation. This is a mobile society—and the college students are no different. Transfers from one college to another are much more prevalent in the Sixties than before. How did one expect loyalty to a large corporate body such as Berkeley or Columbia in this generation? No more than one expected this generation to establish loyalties to a large corporation like IBM. This was not the decade of the Organization Man, but one whose loyalty was directed toward interpersonal relationships rather than absorption within a formal group.

Large group social activities like senior and junior proms have been dying. Barnard College abandoned its senior prom after several years of attempting to perpetuate the tradition with only a handful of takers. Tuxedos and long gowns were seldom seen—gone with them were the bands so popular on campus in the Thirties and even in the Fifties. For this television generation, entertainment might just as happily be a date in a quiet dormitory and a hi-fi set, or a spontaneous guitar folk sing at the quadrangle. A winning team on nationally televised "College Bowl" did not particularly induce the kind of school spirit in the traditional sense.

Rites and events such as Barnard's annual Greek games in which girls paraded in the gymnasium in Greek costumes died also in the Sixties. How many of these nostalgic events like Bryn Mawr's lantern night would remain, and for how long, was the question. The less committed among the students leaving the campuses at vacation time still looked for "beach, broads, and booze" at Fort Lauderdale or "sex, sand, suds, and sun" at Daytona Beach. For Ivy Leaguers and East Coast types the "in" places were the Bahamas, Virgin Islands, San Juan, Guadeloupe, and Tobago. Midwesterners went skiing at Aspen and Taos, while West Coast students skied at Mammouth Mountain in the Sierras.

But times were changing in the Sixties. Added to the normal pleasures pursued by college students during the spring recess of the middle Sixties were activities of serious purpose. Hundreds of students went South, not to vacation at the beaches, but to help rebuild bombed Negro churches or run remedial teaching programs. In California a group of students took as their cause the migrant worker in the

North Central Valley, and tried to help unionize the workers.

An attempt to establish meaningful relationships was a strong undercurrent in the youth of the Sixties, whether these relationships were between student and college, student and teacher, or student and someone of the opposite sex. For the young radicals this meant the need to destroy or attempt to destroy certain customs, mores, or institutions in order presumably to build more meaningful relationships. The young radicals—and probably most of the college generation of the late Sixties—were against what they viewed as the hypocrisies of society. They desired openness and honesty about everything, including sex.

Whether or not there has been much more premarital sex on campus than in earlier decades, a greater openness about the whole matter developed. As the director of counseling and psychological services at Texas said, "They have gone beyond sex . . . They are interested in relationships with people of which sex is a part."

The New York Times ran an article about college students of the opposite sex openly keeping house together. As a result of this article, the Barnard College administration discovered that one of its students was living with a boyfriend from Columbia. Upon further investigation, it appeared that the girl was given permission to live off campus because she had claimed that she had a live-in babysitting job with a family. The disciplinary committee after an agonizing review of the case found the girl guilty of falsifying her record and punished her by removing certain campus social privileges from her. The following letter to President Martha Peterson from a famous alumna, Mrs. Edward L. (Doris Fleischman) Bernays, class of 1913, put the problem of adult hypocrisy in perspective and showed that it went beyond one incident in importance:

Dear President Peterson:

As a Barnard Alumna of the Class of 1913, and as a professional student of the effect of institutional action on the public mind, I suggest that your way of dealing with the problem of Miss ——— has been damaging to the College. I believe it has also been damaging to higher education. Peripherally, and centrally, Barnard is guilty of implied falsehood and disingenuous in stating that Miss _____ may be stigmatized and asked to leave because she "admittedly falsified her record with the College so that she might share an apartment with a Columbia junior."

Many people might argue that lying is an integral part of our culture and one of its conventions. People habitually tell little lies, white lies, social lies, eleemosynary lies, selfish lies, kind lies, vicious lies, military lies, official lies, expedient lies— lies to fit innumerable kinds of situations and for innumerable reasons, including the natural desire for privacy. It would be interesting, but unimportant to the cause of truth-telling, to know whether this Barnard student, in order to spare her parents' distress or anger, lied cynically, desperately, or out of love.

Moreover, since she is acting in imitation of the prevalent behavior of our society, I cannot believe that this student's negation of the values you cite in your Report as "honor and personal integrity", threatens either Barnard College or what we like to think of as our ethical standards.

My second major disagreement with the expressed policy of Barnard has to do with the yoking of two disparate ideas in an oxymoron in order to arrive at an unwarranted conclusion. You say, "She falsified her record with the College so that she might share an apartment with a Columbia junior." Is the accused student to be punished for falsifying her record? Or for living in sin, known in classical terminology as fornication? If the first charge is true, one would, I think, be forced to punish every student, and parent, and legislator, and diplomat. Everyone, in short. No sane person never lies.

If she is to be punished for fornication, it would be best to face the issue and deal with it frankly and intelligently. To do this would entail some considerable research into social history and social sciences and demand that we lock out, among other things, the stale, boring, but annoyingly persistent question of the double standard. What, by the way, is the Columbia junior . . . likely to encounter in the way of censure or career penalties?

There are, of course, many ways of looking at boy and girl rebellion. But there has never been a way of eliminating boys and girls in love. We might make the whole subject less debasing to all of us, and more wholesome in the societal pattern, if we were to act in situations such as the present one with more intelligence and compassion.

Obviously, the role of college president is more taxing today than it has ever been in the history of education. I hope you will find a better way through this morass.

> Sincerely yours,
> Doris Fleischman Bernays

It seemed that the student of the Sixties was entirely different from the student of previous decades. An older graduate looking at this period was inclined to say that in his own day there was more scholarship. But actually more was demanded of the undergraduate in the Sixties in terms of scholarship than his predecessor of a decade or two earlier. He was expected to know more when he entered college and was expected to be able to do more on his own.

The exhilaration of joining demonstrations and sit-ins did not take precedence over the need to finish term papers and prepare for examinations. One was surprised by the number of textbooks carried into the all night sit-in and sleep-ins. In fact, demonstrations all but ceased during examination periods. For the most part these students were not revolutionaries, they simply desired change. If the

Fifties was an age of consolidation, the Sixties became an age of action. And it became an age of action because change was possible.

Beginning with President Kennedy in 1961, there arose a sense that change was possible. The success of the sit-ins in the South was proof of that. The desire for change was the ethos of the early Sixties, whether it was by working as a volunteer in the ghettoes, marching in Selma, registering blacks in the South, or sitting in at Woolworths.

After the Berkeley affair, it appeared that the traditional structure of the American university could be changed. The acceptance of student evaluation of professors, the abolishing of the grading system, the loosening up of requirements for graduation, and the development of more "relevant" courses were no small victory for students of the Sixties. By the late Sixties, a more profound structural change was taking place. Undergraduates became voting members on important committees and finally on Boards of Trustees.

By 1970, the Columbia University policy-making Senate, with 23 student members out of 101, voted against the university participating in secret research with the government or private industry. M.I.T. had already converted its research program from war-oriented to urban problems.

Indeed students were in a position to overwhelm the university, if not the whole of society. As Stephen Spender said, "Previously it was reasonable to assume that the buildings of the older universities—with all they symbolize —influenced the students. Today, it would be truer to say that the students crowd out the buildings."

The students of the Sixties searched hard for meaning in their lives and for a sense of belonging. They sought to find themselves through action and emotion rather than reflection. They submerged themselves in the Movement or collective protest action where they found euphoria and unity. At the same time they sought to find themselves in intense relationships with other individuals.

Jack Newfield, the astute editor of the *Village Voice,* suggests that unlike the student radicals of the Thirties, who were nourished on the dogma of Lenin, Marx, and Trotsky, the new student radical of the Sixties was a member of an incoherent and diverse group nurtured by the writings of Herbert Marcuse, C. Wright Mills, Albert Camus, Norman Mailer, Paul Goodman, and Bob Dylan. Without a central focus, the new radicalism was pluralistic to the extent that anarchism, passivism, and socialism mingled in various proportions. It differed from campus to campus and from city to city. The one clear thing that could be said was that it was anti-Establishment, but student radicals sometimes differed even as to the definition of Establishment.

Following the Silent Generation of the Fifties, this student group spoke out on issues that concerned them—and did something about them. Much of, although not all, the protest on campus was aimed at the immorality of the war in Vietnam. Much of the unrest on campuses was aimed at the deprivation of the American black man. Much of the protest was aimed at the problems of alienation in American society, the cult of conformity, the dominance of middle-class values, and the impersonality of urban living. To some extent these values influenced all students of the Sixties.

The alumni of the Sixties' classes will not reminisce about their favorite pranks. They will recall the social issues that concerned them. They will recall the Sixties as years of questioning and uncertainty rather than of happiness and fun.

EPILOGUE

To quote Jack Newfield, "a prophetic minority creates each generation's legend." In the Twenties it was the quest for personal expression. In the Thirties it was radical social action. In the Forties it was heroism in battle. In the Fifties it was privatism. In the Sixties it was once again the ideal of social action that was defining a generation.

The ethos of each generation has evolved not only out of a reaction to the current issues but also out of a concern with conditions for the future, political or social. To designate student behavior simply as a problem or the "generation gap" is to misunderstand grossly the role of youth. As Stephen Spender says, ". . . it would be better to speak not of the generation gap, but rather of an overlap of problems of the future with the day-to-day ones of the present. . . . So the young generation is not so much a 'gap' as an overlapping of the future, burdened with problems, which to the old seem abstract, but which are built into the flesh and blood of the young."

Three sets of issues will most likely dominate the concerns of college students in the future. The scene of the action may shift, repressive measures may quiet the campuses down, and the tactics may change, but injustice, whether it be racial injustice or the death of innocent human beings, will continue to cause youthful indignation as it has in the past.

There is already increasing concern over the deterioration of our environment, aggravated as it is by the population explosion. The pollution of air and water, the inhuman crowding and decay of the inner city, the shortsighted planning of roads and buildings, and the mismanagement of natural resources are compelling issues for those who have a concern for the quality of life in the future. One of the most popular singers, Tom Lehrer, composed "Pollution."

Concern over the progressive depersonalization of American life is a corollary to these issues. The slogan "I am a Berkeley student—Do not bent, spindle, or mutilate" is a haunting commentary on the problem. Recognizing that this is no longer a world in which any one man is indispensable, they wonder if any single individual or even group of individuals can make an impression, much less an impact, on the existing order. To this growing impersonality it is not difficult to predict either numb passivity on the one hand or an aimless lashing out in frustration on the other. We have already experienced the first in the Fifties and the latter in the Sixties, and neither was constructive.

A third set of issues is less easy to define. At its roots is the knowledge explosion, and its symptomatic cry is for "relevance" and a condemnation of narrow specialization. The knowledge explosion has already created a serious problem in the development of a cohesive society. C. P. Snow's *The Two Cultures* defined the problem broadly— but the problem is much more complex than establishing an understanding between the scientists and the humanists. Within a single academic department, especially in the social and behavioral sciences, one can find not only different areas of interests and schools of thought but also totally different methodologies. The Register of Scientific and Technical Personnel classified over 900 distinct scientific and technical specializations compared with 54 listed twenty years ago. Society is demanding and the university is creating more and more specialists. But a specialist must engage in a lifetime of learning and at the same time progressively narrowing the focus of his work, if he is to keep up with his profession. Intellectual fragmentation as well as societal fragmentation makes cohesion virtually impossible, and the undergraduate is caught in the middle of it. The professor—a specialist—is further removed from undergraduate teaching.

There are the problems of the Seventies. Students are already aware of them, although their anxiety may not always express itself in the most articulate, constructive, or direct manner.

All of us are guilty of saying to our friends, colleagues, or children, "In my college days . . ." Sometimes we are referring to a happier, more carefree, time when we were involved in having a ball or doing our thing. At other times, it is to moralize about the present generation, by comparing it with our presumably saner, more law-abiding, conscientious, respectful generation.

Each decade ends with the current generation of college students being credited as brigher, better trained, and more promising than the previous generation. Yet an age of innocence seems to come to an end in each period.

Each generation discovers its own gods, its own high priest, its own answers. Each generation grapples in its own way with the problems of war, injustice, sex, and job security. And through its struggles with these, each generation defines its own ethos.

BIBLIOGRAPHICAL NOTES

The author is deeply indebted to a great number of writers for their insight and information on student life in the twentieth century.

There are several histories of American higher education that were helpful in providing the background for student life. Frederick Rudolph's *The American College and University* is an excellent book that unfortunately covers only up to the 1930s. John S. Brubacher and Willis Rudy's *Higher Education in Transition* covers from the Colonial period to the 1950s and was also quite useful.

There are hundreds of histories of American colleges and universities. Unfortunately most institutional histories do not give much treatment to student life. They usually cover such subjects as the presidents who lead their institutions, the increases in enrollment over the years, and the number of new buildings that have been built. Those that were particularly helpful were: *A History of Cornell* (1962), by Morris Bishop; *A History of the University of Mississippi* (1949), by Allen Cabaniss; *The University of Utah, a History of its First 100 Years, 1850–1950* (1960), by Ralph Vary Chamberlin; *A Hundred Years of Mount Holyoke College: The Evolution of an Educational Ideal* (1940), by Arthur Charles Cole; *Columbia, Colossus on the Hudson* (1947), by Horace Coon; *A History of the University Founded by John Hopkins* (1946), by John C. French; *Syracuse University* (1952), by William Freeman Galpin; *The First Century at the University of Washington, 1861–1961* (1961), by Charles Marvin Gates; *University of the Northern Plains, a History of the University of*

North Dakota, 1883–1958 (1958), by Louis George Geiger; *Wellesley: Part of the American Story* (1949), by Alice Payne Hackett; *Michigan State: The First 100 Years, 1855–1955* (1955), by Madison Kuhn; *Rutgers: A Bicentennial History* (1966), by Richard Patrick McCormick; *Light on the Hill; A History of Tufts College, 1852–1952* (1966), by Russell E. Miller; *Stanford: The Story of a University* (1959), by Edith Ronald Mirrielees; *Yale College: An Educational History, 1871–1937* (1952), by George Wilson Pierson; *History of Ohio State University: The Story of its First Seventy-five Years, 1873–1948* (1952), by James Edward Pollard; *Vassar Women: An Informal Study* (1940), by Agnes Rogers; *Michigan, The Story of the University* (1948), by Kent Sagendorph; *The University of Kentucky* (1965), by Charles Gano Talbert; *The Ball State Story: From Normal Institute to University* (1967), by Glenn White.

Magazines in the first half of the twentieth century were often good sources for information on student life. *The Literary Digest* was particularly useful. Also helpful were *Scribner's, Saturday Evening Post,* the *Woman's Home Companion, The Nation, Harper's Weekly,* and the *New Republic. Fortune Magazine,* which began in the Thirties, ran at least one very comprehensive article on college students during each decade. *Time* magazine was useful in spotting events in higher education from the Thirties to the present. And, of course, one depended heavily upon *The New York Times.*

For the period from 1900 through the Twenties, Mark Sullivan's six volumes entitled *Our Times* provided a great deal of general history of the times. *The Little Magazine* by Frederick J. Hoffman, Charles Allen, and Carolyn F. Ulrich was an important source of information on the literary thrust of the period. William Leuchtenburg's *Perils of Prosperity: 1914–1932* and Henry May's *End of American Innocence* also provided useful insights. Frederick Lewis Allen's *Only Yesterday* and *Since Yesterday* were very helpful informal histories.

Charles Merz's *The Dry Decade* (1931) is a standard work on prohibition and Andrew Sinclair's *Era of Excess* was also

helpful. James Wechsler's *Revolt on the Campus* remains not
only one of the finest treatments of student radicalism of the
Thirties but also of the Twenties. Murray Kempton's *Part of
Our Time: Some Monuments and Ruins of the Thirties* (1955)
and *As We Saw the Thirties* edited by Rita James Simon provided general insights on the Thirties.

Paul Sann's book entitled *Fads and Follies* was a convenient
source for some of the college fads. *The Age of Rock* edited by
Jonathan Eisen was useful on the recent music scene.

For the chapter on the Fifties, I found very helpful: Eric F.
Goldman's *The Crucial Decade and After* and Alfred McClung
Lee's *Fraternities Without Brotherhood.*

Of the vast amount of material published on student unrest
in the Sixties, I found the following books of great value: *A
Prophetic Minority* by Jack Newfield; *Young Radicals* by
Kenneth Keniston; *Up Against the Ivy Wall* by Jerry L. Avorn
and Robert Frichman; *Crisis at Columbia,* the report by the
Cox Commission; *Education at Berkeley* by the Select Com-
mittee on Education; *The Berkeley Student Revolt* edited by
Seymour Martin Lipset and Sheldon S. Wolin; *Teach-Ins,
U.S.A.,* edited by Louis Minashe and Ronald Radosh; and *The
New Radicals* by Paul Jacobs and Saul Landau.

Various books on the movies, drama, music, dancing, and
the social scene were scanned. The annual almanacs—*The
World, Information Please,* the *Reader's Digest,* and *The New
York Times*—were indispensable in checking titles and dates.
And no author of social history could do without *70 Years of
Best Sellers* by Alice Payne Hackett.